THE
COGNITIVE
ENRICHMENT
ADVANTAGE
Teacher Handbook

Katherine H. Greenberg

KCD Harris & Associates
PO Box 16381
Knoxville, TN 37996

Published by
KCD Harris & Associates Press
PO Box 16381
Knoxville, TN 37996
USA

Originally published by SkyLight Training and Publishing Inc., © 2000

Greenberg, Katherine H.
The Cognitive Enrichment Advantage Teacher Handbook

Includes references, glossary and index.
    1. Cognitive Education. 2. Strategic Thinking.
    3. Teaching and Learning—Integral Educational Approach.
    4. Learning to Learn. 5. Teachers—Theoretical Framework.

ISBN 0-9768095-0-8

Acknowledgment

I wish to acknowledge with much gratitude the mentoring of Reuven Feuerstein over the past twenty-nine years. The dedicated work of many teachers in many lands sharing their ideas and the early and ongoing support and assistance from Janice Wilder, Cynthia M. Gettys, and Teresa J. O'Fallon have deeply enriched me as well as the Cognitive Enrichment Advantage (CEA). I will always appreciate the wonderful team efforts of Follow Through Program Staff Rosa Kennedy, Cheryl Bynum, Kim Graham, and Sandra Machleit and the valuable action research efforts of Gail Collins. I am equally grateful to the ideas and support from CEA consultants, including my sister Carol A. Harris, Lisa Chase-Childers, Irene Mooney, Donna Wilson, Janet Jones and the Detroit team of the United States, Lorna Williams and others in the Vancouver Schools in Canada, Bea Fisher and others with corrective education in Canada, Willie Rautenbach and other educators in South Africa, Carlina Valke and Jaime Valenzuela Salazar and the team from Universidad Catolica del Maule in Talca, Chile, and Johnan Warnez and the staff of the Centrum Voor Het Bevorderen Van De Cognitieve Ontwikkeling vzw in Belgium. Finally, the inspiration of my husband, Neil Greenberg, and daughters, Lisa Michelle Kopp and Haley Jessica Greenberg, means the world to me.

Contents

CHAPTER 4

Integrating Metastrategic Knowledge into the School Curriculum 119

CHAPTER 5

Reflecting on Cognitive Enrichment Advantage Use 151

Preface

In almost thirty years of working—and learning—in cognitive education, I have come to believe that we need to create a radically different learning environment from the traditional one.

Traditional teaching methods, where the teacher attempts to transmit to students most of the information they need, are no longer effective. I believe this statement is true whether these methods are used in kindergarten or graduate school. Some students, although not nearly as many as one would hope, do graduate from high school and the university. But complaints are increasing about the capacity of some of these graduates to find success in the workplace. Further, consensus is building around a different view of what learning is and how it takes place, ways that are not as well nurtured by traditional teaching methods.

We have entered the Information Age. In this age, each of us needs more than ever to think flexibly as we deal with continually changing and evermore-complex information. We need to know how to construct our knowledge by combining the new information we receive with what we already know, sometimes rejecting some of the new or some of the old. More education experts believe we must accomplish this form of learning socially through interaction with others. As information and technology bring societal changes in more frequent and major ways, and as we move toward a global society, which also increases the complexity, educators can no longer predict today what their students—or they—will need tomorrow. Even those who excel at teacher-centered traditional learning need more explicit knowledge about how to learn in the Information Age. In fact, both teachers and learners must have explicit knowledge—clear and exact understanding about how to learn—to ensure that effective learning takes place.

The goal of the Cognitive Enrichment Advantage (CEA), previously known as COGNET, is to teach learners how to learn. The premise of this teaching and learning approach is that learners who understand how they learn are able to develop personal learning strategies that can help them cope with any new learning situation. Further, teachers and learners who understand how best to facilitate learning realize the critical importance of one's personal worldview and cultural beliefs as the foundation for the development of learning potential.

When federal funding for CEA began (1988–1991), it was in use in one school in a rural, Appalachian setting in east Tennessee. In this school, every classroom was a highly traditional learning environment; even kindergarten teachers lectured primarily and drilled students on rote memory tasks, albeit briefly. Students spoke when called on to state the one right answer; otherwise, teachers expected them to work quietly without talking to other students.

The goal of CEA is to create a learning environment in which there is not one right answer, an environment in which students speak more than the teacher does, especially to each other. I wanted to create a laboratory for learning in the classroom where all members of the classroom community, including the teacher, are learners who explore the world together in personally relevant ways. Together, they socially construct knowledge through interaction with others while focusing on the process of learning at least as much as the product. In this way, students learn explicitly how to learn in all kinds of situations. When problems arise for one or more learners, the teacher and other students mediate learning experiences in ways that do not deprive anyone of the opportunity to learn. For example, if a student has difficulty working a math problem, others do not immediately demonstrate how to compute the answer. Instead, the teacher or other students ask questions that focus on the process of learning in this situation. They encourage the learner to develop a strategy for approaching the problem based on one of CEA's Building Blocks of Thinking or Tools of Learning. These mediators do not provide a strategy and do not demonstrate how to work the math problem unless all attempts to help the learner function independently have not brought about success. It was clear my view of an effective learning environment was not compatible with the traditional view of the teachers in this rural Appalachian school.

With almost no knowledge at the time of how to facilitate change, my intuition told me I needed to respect the teachers' methods for establishing a learning environment. So initial CEA teacher workshops focused on cognitive processes and affective-motivational approaches to learning, CEA Building Blocks of Learning and Tools of Learning. The teachers saw these as "thinking skills."

When the teachers returned to their classrooms and shared the thinking skills with their students, they were surprised at how quickly students developed their own learning strategies. Because of the focus on rote drill and practice workbook pages, students had little need for learning strategies in school, but they told their teachers how they were using them in situations outside of school. In addition, data collected confirmed that these teachers were displaying more characteristics of high quality mediated learning. In other words, these teachers engaged students in interactions with the intent to energize the learning experience and helped students become mindful of the learning process that led to success. Similarly, teachers displayed high quality mediated learning if they helped students find inner meaning or personal value for the learning experience or focused students' attention on any

Building Block of Thinking or Tool of Learning and its usefulness in the learning experience.

At the beginning of the second year, CEA consultants shared with the teachers more information about the kind of classroom environment that facilitates learning more readily than a traditional environment. For example, good teachers often tell students what they need to know. Teacher-mediators more frequently collaborate as another learner with students to reflect about what each person already knows and see how this knowledge connects to new information. Good teachers often isolate specific concepts for teaching. Teacher-mediators also connect concepts to students' real-world experiences. Consultants did not point out the differences between the current environments and the new nor did they insist that teachers change their classroom environments. Within a few months, however, we began to see teachers experimenting with different teaching methods that engaged students in more challenging activities. By the third year, teachers asked CEA staff for computer activities in which students work together to solve difficult problems. Within a short time, their students were using software and completing activities usually reserved for students two or three grades beyond their level. Further, a consultant to the project reported that these students were learning to work in small groups much more quickly than were students she had observed who had not learned how to learn explicitly. Data revealed that the students participating in CEA made gains in academic achievement that were much greater than those of the comparison group.

Encouraged by these small successes, CEA obtained additional federal support to expand the program to five new school partnerships. A comparison of events at each of the five schools revealed that the change process occurred more successfully for teachers who had more frequent and better opportunities to explore and reflect together on their experiences in the classroom. This collaborative learning among teachers was more important than the opportunities CEA consultants provided for review of program concepts. At our annual Leadership Forums, participants requested more time to engage in focused conversations with other practitioners from many different schools and less time to listen to the "experts" share additional formal knowledge.

The change in the workshop structure mirrored changes in my teaching methods both in the workshops and in my graduate courses. I have moved from seeing myself as the sole provider of knowledge to becoming a facilitator of knowledge sharing by all participants. During workshops, I still monitor the development of skills related to each objective, but I have relinquished control over the process by which participants master objectives, which is now up to the group at large. I encourage all participants to share information that might help each of us develop a better understanding of some aspect of CEA. Although I provide some of this information myself, I also become another learner in the group, often taking as many notes as others on information shared or insights we develop together. I work hard to help participants feel comfortable in experimenting with the model and encourage them to offer ideas that might improve the model.

When I began the development of CEA, I thought the best way to solve problems in education was to put theory into practice. I have learned that problem solving is not that simple. Peter Jarvis (1992), Professor of Adult Education, University of Surrey, helped me gain an explicit understanding of what I have been learning through experience: People do not learn or create change by putting theory into practice—they learn by deriving theory from practice. In other words, when they see formal theory as relevant to their professional practice, they experiment with it in practice and integrate it into what they already know implicitly. To reflect deeply and to integrate new ideas or formal theories fully, these practitioners must make personal, implicit theories explicit. Effective learning and change occur only when practice is reflective or influenced by "sustained inquiry into the relationship between thought and action" (Peters 1991, 90). In other words, teachers need opportunities to talk with one another about what they believe and how they act on their values in the classroom. To be sure, formal theories can and should influence sustained inquiry. However, as I work with teachers, parents, and others in long-term partnerships, I find their reflective practice and personal theories improve CEA immensely and have turned it into an open system, designed to be modified for use according to the needs of each and every setting. I do not draw on the standard view of higher education, which holds that learning is based on a cognitive under-standing of knowledge. According to Bruffee, this traditional approach assumes that knowledge is "an entity that we transfer from one head to another" (1993, 199). CEA's approach is that knowledge is "a consensus among the members of a community of knowledgeable peers—something people construct by talking together and reaching agreement" (Bruffee, 199). Collaborative learning is critically important if Lev Vygotsky, Reuven Feuerstein, and a growing number of others are correct that knowledge is socially constructed. If society faces continuous change, its future may well depend on educators' ability to help all students, especially those who are not as yet reaching their full potential.

It is my experience that many learners have been falling between the cracks. In the past, these learners could find a job and make a living to support a family. Today, however, jobs change frequently. Even low level workers need good thinking skills. Thus, the future of society depends on reaching all students. Teachers and theorists alike are exploring important new dimensions of teaching and learning. William A. Henry III (1992, 36) states society's need clearly in his comments on the next century:

[T]he urgency of making collaborative decisions about the [world's] environment, tech-nology, and natural resources will compel new ways of working together. The tribal must

give way to the global. People everywhere are going to have to . . . demand much more from themselves. For the future to be bright, it must be lit by the lamp of learning, the true Olympic torch.

The lamp of learning is complex and includes cognition, affect, and motivation as seen through the eyes of each person's culture. The demands people make of themselves must include the ability to learn to learn, to think more deeply, and to understand the importance of integrating cognition, affect, and motivation in all learning. Moving from the tribal to the global depends on each person's ability to make the implicit, tribal understanding explicit enough to integrate with the global. As people from many tribes interact together, society will need love and trust to be successful. In *The Fourfold Way,* Arrien translates a passage from Octavio Paz's *The Labyrinth of Solitude*:

> What sets worlds in motion is the interplay of differences. . . . By suppressing differences and peculiarities, by eliminating different civilizations and cultures, progress weakens life and favors death. The ideal of a single civilization for everyone implicit in the cult of progress and technique impoverishes and mutilates us. Every view of the world that becomes extinct, every culture that disappears, diminishes a possibility of life! (Arrien 1993, 147)

CEA is about making the implicit knowledge explicit. As society moves from the tribal to the global, it must not give up the tribal. CEA can help teachers address the personal worldview and cultural beliefs of every student.

Since that first experience in a rural Tennessee elementary school, the success of CEA has validated its comprehensive mediated learning teaching method and ramified into areas I could not have imagined. I find myself traveling to many places and learning from many people in widely varying settings. CEA has been implemented in classrooms in California, Massachusetts, Michigan, Nebraska, New York, North Carolina, Oklahoma, Tennessee, and Maryland as well as in Belgium, Brazil, Canada, Chile, the Netherlands, and, most recently, South Africa. These locations and their inhabitants, for all their differences, have something very important in common: all face change in the new millennium. Dealing with these changes requires flexibility of mind and the capacity not only to adapt to new situations but also to make changes vital to the survival of the world.

Wherever CEA is used, its vision is to help students become effective, independent, lifelong learners who are able to adapt to an ever-changing world, to make good decisions about their relationships with the world, and to make this world a better place.

INTRODUCTION

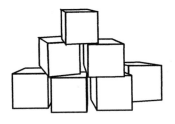

What Is the Cognitive Enrichment Advantage?

The Cognitive Enrichment Advantage (CEA) was founded in 1984 under the name COGNET and expanded for school use in 1988 to provide teachers with skills to help underachieving students learn how to learn. CEA, which draws on the theoretical work of clinical psychologist Reuven Feuerstein, Lev Vygotsky, and others, is a comprehensive teaching method of practices in cognitive education that have been demonstrated as effective (Greenberg, Woodside, and Brasil 1994; Greenberg, Machleit, and Schlessmann-Frost 1996). CEA helps students develop personal learning strategies based on explicit knowledge of twelve cognitive processes that help them think effectively and eight affective-motivational approaches to learning that help them become independent and interdependent learners. Further, the model describes the important role teachers and family members play as mediators of learning experiences and how they can create learning environments that facilitate reflective and critical thinking.

A Metastrategic Approach to Learning to Learn

The CEA comprehensive teaching method differs in an important way from many other cognitive education approaches. A metastrategic approach, it goes beyond cognitive and even metacognitive approaches.

Cognitive teaching methods focus on student acquisition of learning strategies designed by experts to apply to specific tasks such as reading comprehension or mathematics problem solving. Research on this type of approach reveals that students can learn the strategies but might have difficulty applying the strategies to other learning situations, even to similar classroom tasks (Ashman and Conway 1997). Ashman and Conway suggest that the strategies may not have personal relevance for students, and, hence, students use them only under teacher supervision. In addition, this kind of cognitive education approach may omit instruction on self-monitoring use of the strategy or determining the need for the strategy in a new situation. Metacognitive approaches in cognitive education overcome the latter problem by teaching students how to plan and monitor the use of the learning strategy; however, these approaches do not address the personal relevance issue. In CEA's metastrategic approach, students develop the knowledge needed to construct their own personally relevant strategies in any learning experience where they need to do so. The strategies are based on metastrategic knowledge derived from theory and research.

Theoretical Framework

Both theory and research support all practices recommended in CEA. The work of Israeli clinical psychologist and theorist Reuven Feuerstein (Feuerstein et al. 1980), Jean Piaget (1976), Lev Vygotsky (1978), Shirley Brice Heath (1983), and others have greatly influenced CEA.

Piaget refers to the construction of knowledge by individuals primarily through assimilation and accommodation that occurs in response to direct stimuli. Children's cognitive development depends on their opportunities to construct knowledge through their interaction with stimuli in the environment. Vygotsky and Feuerstein maintain that knowledge is socially constructed. Their views of the social construction of knowledge center on the role of a mediator who intercedes in the direct exposure to stimuli to provide meaning that otherwise would not be available to the learner.

The theories of Vygotsky and Feuerstein enhance each other in important ways. Vygotsky describes the zone of proximal development, where one can see the buds of development of human competence within a learner. Vygotsky defines the zone of proximal development as "the distance between the actual developmental level as determined by independent problem solving and the level of potential development as determined through problem solving under adult guidance or in collaboration with more capable peers" (86). Feuerstein's theory of mediated learning experience describes what happens within the zone of proximal development from the perspective of the mediator who assists the learner in moving through the zone and from the perspective of the learner who is developing competence within the zone.

Mediation is a special type of interaction in which one person assists another in learning what the learner would not be capable of learning without this assistance. Feuerstein describes the occurrence of mediated learning as when a more knowledgeable person prompts a less knowledgeable person to label, compare, categorize, and give meaning to a present experience as it relates to prior and future ones. Mediation promotes flexibility of mind and results in learners learning how to learn.

The Cognitive Enrichment Advantage Teacher Handbook focuses on the role of the teacher-mediator within the zone of proximal development. When students receive high quality mediated learning, they learn how to learn, at least implicitly. In CEA and other applications of Feuerstein's theory, however, the knowledge about how one learns becomes explicit for both teacher-mediators and learners. In CEA, it becomes explicit, first, through the use of a shared vocabulary within the learning community for specific cognitive processes and affective-motivational approaches to learning and, second, by teaching students to use these ways of learning to develop learning strategies for any situation. Specific cognitive processes, which

CEA calls Building Blocks of Thinking, are prerequisites to effective thinking. They focus on approaching the learning experience, making meaning of the learning experience, and confirming the learning experience. For example, one Building Block of Thinking, Precision and Accuracy, focuses on becoming aware of the need for precise understanding and accurate use of words and concepts. When learners use this Building Block, they are better able to confirm that they understand a learning experience and ensure that their work is clear and correct. Affective-motivational approaches, or Tools of Learning in CEA, are prerequisites to effective independent and interdependent learning. They focus on understanding feelings and motivating behavior within the learning experience. For example, one Tool of Learning, Inner Meaning, focuses on the need for learners to seek a reason for learning that adds personal value to the learning experience. When learners understand the feelings that come from Inner Meaning, they can energize their learning experiences and improve their ability to learn. A thorough discussion of Building Blocks of Thinking and Tools of Learning appears in chapter 3.

Other research that influences CEA includes the work of Stanford professor Heath, which explains the pervasive influence of language on the development of intelligence and the ways in which one engages in inquiry (1983). The work of Sylvia Weir (1989) at the Technical Education Research Centers in Cambridge, Massachusetts, demonstrates that providing learners of any age with opportunities to inquire, rather than merely memorize, is not enough. Effective learning occurs when learners understand how to learn.

Who Benefits from CEA?

CEA is a comprehensive, schoolwide approach to cognitive education. While it was created to address the needs of schools in low-income areas and, in particular, the needs of underachieving and nontraditional students—students who do not possess the mainstream culture for the given school or community, who are of different ages than their peers, who speak different languages, or who have had significantly different learning experiences than their peers—its concepts are easily adapted for any students in any educational setting. Intended for use by regular and special program teachers, professional support staff, and paraprofessionals, the classroom component can serve as an intervention approach with nontraditional and underachieving students or a preventive approach to forestall learning and behavior problems that often accompany underachievement and nontraditional learning situations as well as bad learning that can occur with all types of learners.

CEA Implementation History

CEA began as a pilot project under the name COGNET with preschool staff at the Douglas Cherokee Economic Authority Head Start Agency in east Tennessee in 1984. In 1988, the original COGNET teaching method underwent revisions and expanded to become one of fifteen national Follow Through education models for young students at risk for school failure: the U.S. Department of Education awarded several million dollars of support to COGNET research and implementation projects at the University of Tennessee, Knoxville, and several field sites. Through these grants, elementary schools in Tennessee and on the Flathead Indian Reservation in Montana worked as partners with university staff to demonstrate use of the model in four urban and two rural schools. COGNET remained one of the national education models until Follow Through's termination by the federal government in 1995 (USDE grants #S014C10013 and #S014C11013).

CEA has been implemented in a variety of cultural, linguistic, and socioeconomic settings throughout the United States and Canada and in other countries, including urban and rural elementary schools that serve students of diverse ethnic backgrounds. In 1997, it became a part of the instructional model for educators working with adults in prison schools in several Canadian provinces. A teacher handbook and related materials have been translated into Flemish, Portuguese, and Spanish.

Evaluation of CEA Use in Schools

Throughout CEA's implementation, the model has undergone continuous evaluation through a variety of formal and informal methods, including ongoing interaction with school staff implementing the model. The information gathered has been used to determine the most effective approaches for professional development activities as well as to refine CEA materials, such as this handbook. In 1995, a proposal to the U.S. Department of Education described fourteen research studies undertaken to assess the effect of this cognitive education program on student academic achievement and teacher classroom behavior in rural and urban schools. The Education Department's National Diffusion Network Performance Effectiveness Panel reviewed the study results and awarded CEA its approval as an education program with demonstrated effectiveness.

CEA staff at the University of Tennessee, Knoxville, has conducted several evaluation studies. A detailed report of these research studies and a summary of other research are available from the University of Tennessee.

A major, seven-year series of research studies (1988–1995) examined the effects of CEA on academic achievement of elementary school students in a variety of settings.

Students considered at risk for academic failure who attended schools using CEA for two or more years made greater gains overall on standardized achievement tests than comparison groups (Greenberg, Machleit, Schlessmann-Frost 1996). These students exceeded gains expected based on national norms and gains in National Curve Equivalency scores (NCEs). CEA schools also displayed significant decreases in the percent of students scoring below average on achievement tests as the students moved from first to fourth grade. In 1991, 72 percent of cohort students in one CEA school scored below average in reading. By 1994, only 48 percent scored below average in reading. In a comparison school, 44 percent scored below average in reading in 1991, and by 1994, 57 percent scored below average. These studies took place in urban and rural settings in Tennessee. Reliability of the results is enhanced by data reported for several cohorts of environmentally and ethnically different groups of students in four different treatment schools during two different time periods (1988–1991 and 1991–1994). All four studies used comparison groups in an attempt to control for the change in student data possibly attributed to maturation. All comparison groups were matched to their treatment groups based on grade level, geographic location, characteristics of the families served within the school, and participation in designated Title I Schoolwide Project Schools.

Several other positive findings have emerged from CEA impact studies. In one study in a rural elementary school and its comparison school, data were collected on measures of intrinsic motivation and cognitive functioning. CEA students made significantly higher gains than the comparison group. Through journal writings from a wide variety of schools, students have demonstrated a high level of internalization and ability to transfer CEA concepts. In addition, students in one school who displayed limited English proficiency reversed a long-term trend of decreasing academic achievement scores by demonstrating gains in eight of thirteen areas tested after two years of participation in the CEA program. These students were Native Americans whose grandparents had been sent to mission schools where they had been deprived of their own language but had not been able to learn English well. As a result, their own children and grandchildren had limited English proficiency. Hence, almost all Native Americans on this reservation were considered to have limited English proficiency even though few can speak the native language.

A second body of research was designed to study the effects of CEA on teachers' ability to facilitate higher-order thinking and learning skills through the use of a mediated learning teaching method. One study compared teachers in four urban schools who had received extensive professional development in the use of CEA with teachers in two urban comparison schools. CEA teachers were characterized as using intent, transcendence, lesson purpose, strategic teaching, and modification in their interactions with students during instructional activities to a greater degree than comparison teachers did. A study of teachers in a CEA rural elementary school and a comparison school revealed higher levels of mediated learning characteristics

on the part of CEA teachers engaged in classroom interactions with students. Although some CEA teachers scored at lower levels of mediated learning (both lower than their colleagues and some of the control teachers), they were not characterized by variables that appear to inhibit high-level mediated learning. (No control teachers scored at the highest level and no CEA teachers scored at the lowest of the five levels.) Comparison teachers with no CEA training who scored at the same lower levels of mediated learning displayed characteristics that appear to interfere with mediated learning experiences during classroom interactions with students. These teachers allowed other students to respond if the first student called on did not provide an adequate response, or they answered for a student who did not respond quickly. These teachers went on to a new topic after getting a quick response to a question without exploring the topic more deeply by asking more questions or providing some kind of elaboration of the response given by a student.

According to the observational analysis data, teachers' classroom interaction profiles changed after participation in CEA professional development activities. These teachers began to ask many more questions during classroom interactions that required higher-level thinking skills. Unlike comparison group teachers, CEA teachers spent more time with students who gave partial or misguided responses and taught their students to respect each student's opportunity for learning by not blurting out answers.

Research studies related to various aspects of the CEA program continue. An in-depth interview study revealed that CEA family workshops helped family members better understand their role in their children's school education. These parents and guardians reported a clearer understanding than a comparison group of parents of how to assist their children in both school-related and home-related activities and in solving problems. Findings related to the use of CEA in a bilingual (English-Spanish) classroom revealed a highly positive effect on students in their ability to create a laboratory for learning (see chapter 2) in the classroom and in students' ability to relate the Building Blocks and Tools to written expression. (Data was qualitative and mostly anecdotal.) An evaluation of the use of CEA in prison schools in Canada with adult students is planned. A qualitative study is also underway to analyze the experiences of an educational therapist and her students in combining the CEA mediated learning teaching method and Building Blocks and Tools with a comprehensive program for overcoming learning disabilities related to reading and language arts skills.

Implementing CEA

The initial phase of CEA use requires a two-year–minimum commitment. Teachers need at least one year to become proficient in using the comprehensive teaching method. Although individual students begin to become better learners in a short time, improved achievement test scores may not be evident at a schoolwide level until the end of the second year of use. School staff needs to commit to active participation in the Level I and II workshops and weekly or bimonthly support meetings. A minimum of four days of on-site coaching from a CEA consultant is also recommended. In schools with approximately twenty or more teachers, appointment of an on-site project coordinator is highly recommended.

CEA Workshops

The purpose of the Level I workshop is to help teachers socially construct knowledge needed to integrate the CEA program into their classroom or professional practice. Throughout the workshop sessions, the CEA consultant models the classroom teaching method for participants. The workshop is highly interactive and collaborative and focuses participant attention on the process of learning and the need for reflection. Together, participants and the consultant create a community of learners. By engaging in collaborative learning during the workshop—by participating in various group activities through which they explore the use of CEA components, reflect on implications of their use, design lessons using components, and provide feedback to other groups—and by exploring their own and others' assumptions related to each component, workshop participants can learn the following:

❑ to use a mediated learning comprehensive teaching method and understand how it differs from the traditional classroom approach (see chapter 2)

❑ to establish a collaborative atmosphere and select and adapt activities for the classroom that nurture authentic learning and challenge all students; in other words, the classroom becomes a laboratory for learning rather than a stage for producing right answers (see chapter 2). Authentic learning is personally relevant to each student and involves activities that are closely related to real-world activities, experiences, and student needs.

❑ to gain an awareness of each student's personal worldview and encourage its important role in learning (see chapter 2)

❑ to implement effective collaborative and cooperative learning and facilitate the development of student social skills (see chapters 2 and 4)

❑ to help students build insight and a shared vocabulary based on the Building Blocks of Thinking and Tools of Learning (see chapter 3). Teachers can benefit from their own learning and use of Building Blocks and Tools.

❑ to facilitate students' (and teachers') development of personal strategies for use in any learning experience based on recognition of effective and

ineffective use of each Building Block of Thinking and Tool of Learning (see chapters 3 and 4)

❏ to facilitate transfer of learning, especially through the technique of bridging Building Blocks and Tools (see chapter 4)

❏ to avoid co-opting learning opportunities (see chapter 2)

❏ to integrate Building Blocks and Tools into curricular activities (see chapter 4 and *The Cognitive Enrichment Advantage Minilessons*)

❏ to help students understand the purpose of school and what it means to become an effective, independent and interdependent, lifelong learner.

Level I Workshop

The Level I workshop requires 30 to 36 hours. The workshop agenda and the scheduling of sessions depend on specific school needs and the components the school adopts. The active participation of principals, other administrators, and professional support staff in the Level I workshop along with teachers and teaching assistants enhances successful use of CEA. All Level I participants receive *The Cognitive Enrichment Advantage Teacher Handbook, The Cognitive Enrichment Advantage Minilessons,* and *The Cognitive Enrichment Advantage Family-School Partnership Handbook.* The Level I workshop begins the journey of CEA use.

Level II Workshop

Staff development activities during the second year of adoption are personalized to a greater extent than those during the first-year workshop. A certified CEA consultant leads an 18- to 20-hour workshop. Participants bring the materials they received during Level I training. Many schools focus on the use of computers with the CEA program during this workshop along with a more in-depth focus on specific aspects of cooperative and collaborative learning and the Building Blocks and Tools. Staff new to adoption sites in the second year can participate in a Level I workshop offered away from their community or in a workshop facilitated by a local certified consultant on-site in a small-group setting.

Additional Professional Development Activities

CEA consultants offer additional workshops as requested. These might focus on alternative assessment, particularly dynamic assessment, and its integration into the CEA model. Others focus on the development of thematic curricular units or refining one's mediated learning teaching approach. CEA also offers a certification workshop for those who wish to become CEA consultants. Another workshop is designed specifically for school administrators and others who facilitate educational change. CEA Leadership Forums have been especially helpful to educators, administrators, family members, and others who come together from a wide variety of communities to share their successes and challenges and learn from each other.

Organization of the Handbook

The Cognitive Enrichment Advantage Teacher Handbook serves as a guide for teachers as they begin using the CEA comprehensive teaching method to help students learn how to learn. Teachers can explore the ideas presented within its pages and integrate them with their own personal philosophy of teaching. Referring to the handbook, revisiting their responses to the items of self-reflection, and collaborating with other users in support meetings can help teachers become CEA experts, adapting the education model to meet the needs of individual students.

The handbook is divided into five chapters. Chapter 1, The Cognitive Enrichment Advantage Program, describes the program, its components, and its implementation.

Chapter 2, Mediated Learning and a Laboratory for Learning in the Classroom, describes CEA's theoretical base of mediated learning experience and examines the qualities of an effective mediator. It explains how to implement CEA in the classroom by creating a laboratory of learning where all students have the opportunity and support to learn independently and interdependently, where students are respected for all thoughts and actions that demonstrate a need to know, and where the process of learning is valued as much or more than the product.

Chapter 3, A Metastrategic Approach to Learning, outlines the heart and soul of the CEA teaching method. It explains the Building Blocks of Learning—twelve cognitive processes that help students think effectively—and the Tools of Learning—eight affective-motivational approaches to learning that help them become independent and interdependent learners.

Chapter 4, Integrating Metastrategic Knowledge into the Curriculum, provides teachers with practical applications of CEA. It describes CEA minilessons and the techniques of transfer and bridging, shows teachers how to create their own minilessons to meet the needs of their students, and assists teachers in using CEA with such classroom practices as collaborative and cooperative learning.

Reflection plays a vital role in any learning process, and Chapter 5, Reflecting on Cognitive Enrichment Advantage Use, provides teachers and students with the opportunity to reflect on their classroom. The teacher reflection checklists found here give teachers a springboard from which to build on their strengths and overcome their weaknesses as mediators in the learning experience. How has their teaching changed? What more would they like to do? to know? The student reflection sheets ask students to think about their effective use of Building Blocks and Tools.

Handbook Dedication

The Cognitive Enrichment Advantage Teacher Handbook is dedicated to all who desire to help students learn how to learn. It is designed as an aid to those in a teaching role who nurture learners of any age in any kind of learning environment, including teaching assistants, school principals and other administrative staff, school counselors, school psychologists, speech and language pathologists, parents and other family members, museum workers, facilitators of special interest groups for students, and team coaches. While teaching builds on the belief that everyone can learn, its ultimate success depends on creating an atmosphere where learning thrives and students learn how to learn.

THE COGNITIVE ENRICHMENT ADVANTAGE PROGRAM

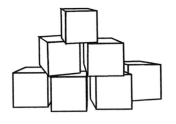

Overview of the Cognitive Enrichment Advantage

At an exponentially increasing pace, society demands that its members act in a responsible manner and function successfully in work and home environments that change continuously (Fullan 1993). So students can meet this demand when they leave school, schools must move away from the traditional view of teachers as transmitters of knowledge who expect students to learn in a linear and sequential way and master surface level, decontextualized skills before moving to challenging, complex, and authentic tasks (Presseisen, Smey-Richman, and Beyer 1993). Instead, teachers must facilitate the learning process, guiding students at all levels through challenging and complex learning experiences and ensuring that students acquire the skills to be successful active and independent learners (Feuerstein et al. 1980; Weir 1989). However, school reform initiatives and achievement test results indicate that students are not acquiring these skills, particularly those students already considered at risk for school failure (National Assessment of Educational Progress 1990).

The Purpose of CEA

The purpose of the Cognitive Enrichment Advantage (CEA) is to establish a school-based community of learners where all students can learn how to learn, become effective lifelong learners, and achieve greater school, social, and career success (see Figure 1.1). To meet these goals, CEA employs three key components:

1. a **comprehensive teaching method** based on mediated learning theory and related ideas. The teaching method combines best practices in cognitive education with a unique focus on the development of a shared vocabulary for metastrategic knowledge that empowers students to create their own learning strategies;

2. a **family-school partnership** that helps family members and school staff work together more closely to meet specific community needs and ensure learner success;

3. a **users' network** that connects teachers and family members in a wide variety of settings to each other and to CEA consultants. The network allows users to share and compare information and experiences related to CEA implementation and to obtain a broader perspective on their successes and challenges.

Comprehensive Teaching Method

CEA is comprehensive because it goes beyond teaching critical thinking skills and learning strategies for specific subject matter study to enable students to create

14

FIGURE 1.1

CEA Long-term Goals

❏ To create a laboratory for learning, a reflective and collaborative atmosphere that enhances independent and interdependent learning and accommodates the social-cultural background of every learner

❏ To apply the theory of mediated learning experience and enhance learning through an explicit understanding of how to ensure the highest quality learning experience

❏ To use Building Blocks of Thinking and Tools of Learning to develop a shared vocabulary among educators, family members, and students that allows all learners to build their own cognitive, affective, and motivational strategies as needed in all learning situations anywhere

❏ To employ CEA as a comprehensive teaching method that enriches best teaching practices for the given school and community based on cultural, family, and individual needs

❏ To create an international, supportive, and expanding network that enables family members, educators, and others to provide and receive mutual support as they seek to maximize learning potential for all students

---

their own learning strategies for any learning situation. It goes beyond the school culture to include the personal worldview and culture of each learner. It goes beyond a teacher-centered or curriculum-centered approach to be student-centered and focus on lessons' value and relevance to the students, culturally and personally. It goes beyond cognition to focus on affect (feelings) and motivation as well.

Because CEA helps students understand the necessity to address affective and motivational needs in learning simultaneously with cognitive needs, CEA is more holistic than many cognitive education approaches that focus solely on critical thinking skills. Affect (feelings) and motivation are as much a part of learning as cognition and may, in fact, interfere with learning more than cognitive processing problems do. Certainly, these two factors can interfere even for those highly gifted in cognitive processing. The foundation of the CEA comprehensive teaching method is the application of the theory of mediated learning experience to enhance learning (Feuerstein et al. 1980) and the creation of a laboratory of learning in the classroom that employs twelve Building Blocks of Learning—cognitive processes that help students think effectively—and eight Tools of Learning—affective-motivational approaches to learning that help students become independent and interdependent learners. (An explanation of the theoretical framework of the CEA teaching method appears in Chapter 2. Chapter 3 describes the Building Blocks and Tools in detail.)

The CEA comprehensive teaching method is designed to be integrated with other best practices and effective curriculum in the classroom. For example, individual schools and CEA teacher-mediators determine for themselves the degree to which they wish to incorporate collaborative and cooperative learning activities with the CEA teaching method. CEA supports teacher development of thematic units and other activities that help students connect lessons with the real world. In schools with the necessary resources, consultants can assist teacher-mediators with techniques that incorporate the comprehensive teaching method with the use of classroom computers. Teacher-mediators learn to select and adapt software that imitates the conditions of real-life experiences so students can work on simulated, yet authentic, and personally relevant projects that integrate the Building Blocks and Tools.

Family-School Partnership

CEA views learning as important in all arenas of life and at all ages and emphasizes the systemic needs of learners, attending to factors in and outside of the classroom that impact learning potential. To support these ideas, CEA includes a family-school partnership, in which school staff, students, and family members share a purpose and use the vocabulary of CEA to work on goals collaboratively.

The family-school partnership component is highly personalized to meet family and school needs. In many schools, family members reinforce the Building Blocks of Thinking and Tools of Learning addressed in the classroom by focusing on their use during everyday activities such as cooking, shopping, planning a party, and doing one's job. Working as equal partners, family members and educators can explore home and school expectations for learning related to Building Blocks and Tools. Together, they can help students develop pride in their home culture, respect for the culture of others, and an understanding of school expectations. Teacher-mediators send home weekly handouts that keep family members informed of the current focus in the classroom and provide suggestions for activities at home. CEA consultants urge schools to provide family members with workshop opportunities to study the teaching method in-depth.

CEA provides a framework for systemic change as it facilitates decision making by school staff and family members. Decisions vary among communities based on community needs and the members of the CEA network. For example, in some CEA schools, users may include only the regular education classroom teachers and principal. Most CEA schools include family members and professional support staff serving the school. Still others also include separate agencies that focus on decisions related to specific community needs (social workers, drug-prevention program staff).

Many CEA schools encourage family members to become active participants with the school. Advisory Boards composed of family members and school staff members

meet regularly, usually monthly. The CEA family-school partnership component offers a wide variety of skill development and volunteer opportunities for parents based on individual, community, and school needs. For example, many schools set up a system for managing and encouraging volunteering by family members. The system includes a plan for how school staff informs volunteer coordinators of its specific needs, a policy for the amount of training a family member receives before engaging in a particular volunteer activity, and coordination of a schedule for volunteer activities. In addition, schools link with health and social service providers and other educational programs to offer parenting classes and other self-improvement activities for family members such as instruction in computer skills or in providing more nutritional meals to their families.

Health and social service needs definitely impact learning: students who have difficulty seeing the board or hearing others speak, experience health problems due to lack of dental care, live in violent and drug-infested neighborhoods, or observe or suffer physical or sexual abuse cannot give adequate attention to learning. Collaboration among families and agencies that provide health services can improve the planning and delivery of these services. Using the school as a central operating place where families can come after school hours for services or information is a helpful option.

Users' Network

CEA consultants establish a long-term, continuous partnership with users. Through these partnerships, CEA provides the following services: 1. coordination of workshops and other professional development activities delivered by certified consultants; 2. sustained technical assistance for schools or agencies as well as assistance by phone, fax, and regular and electronic mail; 3. comprehensive program evaluation; 4. Leadership Forums, which provide opportunities for teachers, administrators, family members, and others to share successes and offer ideas and support for specific challenges; and 5. facilitation of networking activities across communities and schools.

CEA facilitates collaboration within and across schools and their communities as well as between CEA consultants and schools. Facilitating collaboration involves encouraging users to share their ideas and inquire into others' ideas. During the first two years of adoption, CEA consultants help each school establish a system of intraschool and community networks. For example, they set up weekly or bimonthly support meetings for teaching staff and administrators at and beyond the school level and provide suggestions for meeting topics and teacher reflection sessions. Schools and teachers can adapt the networking component to meet their specific needs. For example, some CEA users want very frequent, discuss-anything meetings while others want a more formal, workshop-type follow-up. Some want a consultant to observe in their classrooms to provide direct feedback, and others want this feedback provided only by other teachers with whom they work.

CEA consultants provide technical assistance in the form of help planning project activities and completing data analysis for studies. They encourage business-school partnerships and the creation of Family-School Advisory Boards to provide an opportunity for family leadership in the school. Family leadership is important because the most powerful mediator in a child's life is the person who serves in a parenting role. All learners need to connect their learning to their culture and personal worldviews, and they develop these personal worldviews with or from those closest to them. Those people, whether or not they have the learners' best interests at heart and are responsible in their relationships with the learners, have the greatest influence on learning.

Consultants are also available to facilitate interschool networking. All schools are encouraged to join an electronic network of CEA users. Representatives from schools are strongly encouraged to participate in Leadership Forums.

(Note: For ease of discussion, the handbook uses the term *teacher-mediators* to refer to CEA users; however, users comprise anyone involved in education, including administrators, school counselors and psychologists, and professional and para-professional support staff.)

CEA View of Learners and Learning

CEA is based on important assumptions regarding the individual learner, the role of the teacher-mediator, the context of learning (the circumstances relevant to learning as determined by a view of learning as the social construction of knowledge), and the factors necessary to bring about successful organizational and community change and maximize learning potential. While CEA users vary greatly in their beliefs and values, it is important for them to reflect carefully on the view of learners and learning underlying CEA's comprehensive teaching method to determine if it is compatible with their own assumptions. They must believe that students can learn the vocabulary, understand the concepts, and become independent (to some greater or lesser extent) in developing learning strategies or they will not invest the effort needed to bring change about, and, even more important, they will not convey to learners the expectation for occurrence of effective learning to learn.

Beliefs regarding the individual learner. All human beings, regardless of level of functioning, have a natural and spontaneous desire to learn unless they are in an environment that has taught them to fear learning opportunities. Individuals are members of society within complex environments—individuals have to interact with people who share similar and dissimilar worldviews, deal with popular values vs. those of their ethnic and religious group, and deal with society's expectations for them and their family—and these factors affect their learning. To maximize

learning potential, all individuals need to interact with high quality mediators of their learning experiences who help them relate new ideas to personal experience and make meaning that goes beyond the current learning situation. Individuals learn how to learn when they participate actively in high quality mediated learning experiences. Because mediated learning doesn't occur unless the learner is actively involved and reciprocity exists, a mediator must accept responsibility for encouraging these circumstances as part of high quality mediation.

Beliefs regarding the role of the teacher-mediator. Teachers with an explicit understanding of mediated learning have a framework for decision making regarding its use in the classroom to overcome or prevent learning problems. The primary roles of the teacher-mediator are 1. to become facilitator of a learner-centered and challenging environment that builds on each learner's personal worldview; 2. to create a collaborative, safe, and nurturing learning community within the classroom that provides the support every learner needs to maximize learning potential; and 3. to ensure that everyone within the learning community expects all members to learn, respects all members for their efforts to learn, encourages thinking that leads to effective learning, supports rather than denies learning opportunities for all members, and treats the classroom as a laboratory for learning rather than a stage for producing right answers.

Beliefs regarding the context of learning. First, educators must find ways to prevent learning difficulties, alienation of learners due to race or ethnicity, and poverty from becoming impediments to effective learning. Second, the classroom should be *a laboratory for learning* where the process is emphasized as much as the product, and learners participate in groups that value inquiry over advocacy—exploring their ideas and those of others to reflect on assumptions, expectations, and beliefs that underlie them rather than convincing others to agree that their ideas are best without exploring assumptions—and seek to learn collaboratively. Third, a cognitive enrichment network composed of educators, family members, community representatives, and others must address the systemic needs of learners. Meeting the needs of the student as a whole person requires the entire system working well. When a person has learning problems, family members play a very important role in reinforcing what is going on at school. Professionals with expertise in relevant areas are also needed. If the family has problems that are having an impact, such as abuse, then family members may require professional help before the student can improve.

Beliefs regarding organizational and community change. CEA builds on three premises thought to be critical to the success of change efforts: 1. Schools need to build change efforts on cohesive and sound teaching methods supported by theory, philosophy, and research; 2. School, agency, and community change depends on in-depth and focused professional development opportunities involving long-term partnerships with experts inside and outside the school community who provide technical assistance; 3. Efforts to maximize learning potential succeed best in a collaborative environment with genuine community-inclusive support and ownership, both top-down and bottom-up.

Projected Outcomes of CEA Implementation

CEA is not a quick fix. Its effect on the success of the school community in meeting its vision of improving learner effectiveness can be dramatic, but only if participants devote the time and energy necessary to learn and adapt the model to meet the needs of the given community. Through a minimum two-year period of focused commitment to ongoing professional development and participation in a partnership with CEA administrative staff and certified consultants, schools can meet the projected outcomes that appear in Figure 1.2.

Implementing CEA

A two-year commitment at minimum is needed for the initial phase of CEA use. Teacher-mediators need at least one year to become proficient in using the comprehensive teaching method. School staff needs to commit to active participation in the Level I (approximately 30-hour) workshop, weekly or bimonthly support meetings, and the Level II (approximately 20-hour) workshop. (Also see Figure 1.3 for a list of CEA materials.) CEA also recommends a minimum of four days of on-site coaching by a CEA consultant.

Ideally, school staff and family members implement CEA together, with those in the home reinforcing concepts introduced at school. In addition, CEA recommends the active involvement of school and central office administrators.

CEA consultants suggest that schools in which twenty or more teachers are implementing CEA at the same time designate a CEA project coordinator, a master teacher with collaborative, leadership skills. The project coordinator's duties include coordinating instructional activities, observing and encouraging teachers, demonstrating lessons, planning and conducting weekly or biweekly support meetings for all teaching staff, coordinating the family-school partnership activities, and maintaining links with agencies serving students before and after their enrollment. In situations where only a small number of teachers are implementing the teaching method, an administrator might assume the project coordinator's duties.

CEA consultants also recommend that schools serving a high percentage of students with special learning, health, or social needs designate a comprehensive services coordinator, preferably a licensed social worker with a high level of expertise in working with parents, students, and school staff. The comprehensive services coordinator's duties include facilitating links to health and social services for students

FIGURE 1.2

Projected Outcomes for Schools Implementing the Complete CEA Program

1. Members of the school community work together collaboratively, using CEA to assist them in developing a cohesive and sound educational approach that maximizes student learning potential.

2. School staff and family members possess clear understanding of how learning occurs and methods of increasing learning potential.

3. Classrooms are laboratories for learning where the entire classroom community values the process of learning as much as the product, expects all students to learn, respects them for what they think and say, and never deprives students of a learning opportunity.

4. Teachers adapt school curriculum to meet criteria of the laboratory for learning classroom: activities are relevant to all students, are connected to real-world needs, use technology to engage in challenging simulations of real-life situations that encourage responsible citizenship, engage students in challenging, complex, and authentic tasks, and focus on the process of learning.

5. Teachers act as mediators of learning experience who help students learn how to learn by helping them attend to appropriate information, find meaning in their activities, make connections to past and future situations, and generate their own knowledge.

6. Students possess understanding of basic cognitive processing concepts that foster effective thinking (Building Blocks of Thinking) and affective-motivational approaches that foster independent and interdependent learning (Tools of Learning) and have the ability to construct personal learning strategies based on the Building Blocks and Tools.

7. Students are better able to connect their personal worldviews to the formal knowledge of school and to have pride in their own culture and respect for the culture of others.

8. Family members participate actively on advisory committees and in classroom volunteer programs, in family self-improvement activities, in joint workshops for family members and educators on home and school cultures, and in learning and using a shared vocabulary of Building Blocks and Tools.

9. Health and social service links address the holistic needs of learners and their families.

10. The school is a member of the expanding network of CEA participants worldwide who work together to share effective strategies for achieving the CEA vision and to meet school-based community goals.

and families served by the school, providing crisis intervention and counseling for families and students, and coordinating educational opportunities such as reading or computer literacy classes for family members.

Because CEA is a comprehensive and complex teaching method, most teachers find they need personal initiative, commitment, and, initially, a lot of hard work to develop a feeling of competence regarding integration of CEA into their classrooms (see also Figure 1.4). According to these same teachers, however, the result is

FIGURE 1.3

CEA Materials

CEA materials include the following:

1. *The Cognitive Enrichment Advantage Teacher Handbook:* detailed information on enhancing mediated learning, creating a laboratory for learning in the classroom, integrating the CEA teaching method into regular curriculum activities, using Building Blocks of Thinking and Tools of Learning, and recognizing students' ineffective and effective use of each Building Block and Tool

2. *The Cognitive Enrichment Advantage Minilessons:* ideas for integrating Building Blocks and Tools into four types of learning activities: introductory lessons, group practice and review lessons, independent work, and daily living skills activities

3. *The Cognitive Enrichment Advantage Family-School Partnership Handbook:* information on building successful partnerships as well as explanations for using commonly occurring activities within the home to highlight specific Building Blocks and Tools

4. **Icons** for Building Blocks of Thinking and Tools of Learning to display in the classroom and to reproduce for student use at home (see Appendix)

worth this investment of time and effort. Many teachers express a renewed excitement about teaching and a new perspective on their roles as teacher-mediators, their students' roles as learners, and the role of the classroom environment. These teachers also share a sense of fulfillment as students become empowered as effective, lifelong learners who are able to relate, adapt, and contribute to an ever-changing world in healthy ways.

Monitoring and Evaluation Procedures

CEA offers tools for self-, peer, and supervisory monitoring and evaluation. School staff can monitor and evaluate student performance with traditional and alternative assessment and through diagnostic approaches. CEA consultants can also help evaluate the CEA program's effect on students, school staff, administrators, and family members through methods such as dynamic assessment and conducting observational analysis of classroom interactions.

CEA Management Activities

A high level of resistance to any innovation can be expected unless all participants have the time and opportunity to recognize the need for the change in their environment (Maurer 1996). Everyone from administrators at the top of the system, paraprofessionals and others at the lower level of the system, and teachers and

FIGURE 1.4

Five Levels of User Implementation of Innovative Practices

Based on their observations of many teachers' use of new methods and practices, Hall (1975) describe five levels of implementation of new practices, from novice to expert as outlined below. The CEA program and its system of professional development is designed to help users reach levels four and five where they, as members of a school learning community and on their own, can assimilate and accommodate CEA to the point that they have truly made it their own and, hence, become its experts. A few participants in the Level I workshop reach the integrated use or renewal levels by the end of the workshop, particularly if they have experience with mediated learning. Most participants finish at the orientation level, ready to enter the mechanical use level. To reach these levels of expert use, it is critically important that every user become an active member of a support group, meeting regularly with other users to discuss successes and challenges.

1. **Orientation:** users spend considerable effort planning and preparing for initial use while experiencing little action and effect on current practices;

2. **Mechanical Use:** users rely on feedback and supervision for use in a variety of contexts, make changes more to meet their own rather than student needs, and still need to invest considerable effort planning and preparing, although these activities are less time-consuming;

3. **Routine Use:** users begin to focus less on the details, do not need or want as much feedback and supervision, apply the innovation more easily across contexts, and find planning and preparation need much less effort;

4. **Integrated Use:** users better adapt the innovation to meet the needs of their students based on a clear mental framework for the innovation that fits their personal beliefs and ideas and where planning and preparation take little effort and flow naturally with other activities;

5. **Renewal:** users seek major modifications in or alterations to the innovation based on their need to impact students even more, and they examine new developments in the field and explore new goals for themselves and the school.

other professional staff in-between need to feel they have ownership in the decision to implement change. Personal commitment and ownership build as people become knowledgeable and as they have the opportunity to decide to commit to a new innovation such as the CEA program.

Experience indicates that successful implementation of CEA in schools is enhanced when school staff engage in the following ten management activities:

1. Conduct a school-based needs assessment, develop a shared recognition of needs, and think about outcomes the school hopes to accomplish through the use of CEA.

2. Build awareness and acceptance of CEA policies within the school-based community and provide opportunity for feedback for school staff, school

and central office administrators, family members, professional support staff, and community leaders.

3. Develop a school plan for implementation, including a two-year schedule for goals for implementation of various components of CEA, evaluation activities, staff development activities, ongoing support activities, monthly meetings for those in project leadership roles, and regular feedback meetings for administrators, family members, and other interested community members.

4. Coordinate the presentation of the Level I workshop during the first year for all school staff followed by the Level II workshop in the second year and bimonthly support meetings.

5. Establish an Advisory Board to include representative family members, teachers, support staff, school and central office administrators, and community leaders to facilitate development of a community of learners who can adapt the model to meet specific needs and overcome challenges to successful implementation.

6. Send selected teachers, family members, and staff to CEA Leadership Forums.

7. Arrange for one staff member to become certified as a CEA consultant so the local education agency can expand the use of CEA on its own.

8. Establish a Curricular Review Board made up of teachers and administrators with expertise in selecting curriculum to monitor the selection of classroom materials and the opportunity for staff participation in professional development activities to ensure a theoretically and philosophically cohesive approach to education.

9. Implement early childhood transition activities such as Head Start programs to ensure continuity and quality of services to students.

10. Continually evaluate the process of implementation and revise the program to meet the needs of the given community.

Research and experience demonstrate the critical importance of long-term partnerships between schools involved in change efforts and individuals researching education models. School practitioners cannot ensure that they can achieve goals for serving students and families unless they work collaboratively with experts in theory, research and development, and the facilitation of change. Without this partnership, educational change efforts have no map to guide the way.

Indeed, developers cannot ensure that the approach or program meets the long-term and often difficult needs of individual schools unless they receive continuous feedback over several years from practitioners who are experts on day-to-day implementation and overall management in widely varying situations. Without this expertise, programs and approaches meet few if any real needs. Users are strongly encouraged to arrange for a minimum of two days of on-site follow-up coaching during the first and second year of adoption. CEA staff members use this opportunity to collect feedback from participants to revise workshops and personalize them to meet specific school needs.

The CEA Vision

With the use of mediated learning experiences in an atmosphere that facilitates the social construction of knowledge, CEA maximizes learning potential and nurtures the human spirit in all learners by helping them believe in themselves and their ability to become effective learners. As a result, learners become

- ❏ mindful of the need to learn how to learn explicitly,

- ❏ mindful of the need to employ Building Blocks of Thinking and Tools of Learning,

- ❏ mindful of the need to develop personal learning strategies in challenging situations,

- ❏ mindful of their relationship to the world and to all living things,

- ❏ mindful of what is needed to adapt and contribute to an ever-changing world in healthy ways, and

- ❏ mindful of the need for independent and interdependent, lifelong learning.

Chapter 2

MEDIATED LEARNING AND A LABORATORY FOR LEARNING IN THE CLASSROOM

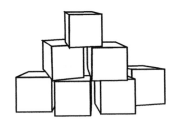

The Process of Learning

Most people learn how to learn naturally, beginning at birth and continuing throughout life, but most do not have explicit knowledge of how they learn or how to help themselves become better learners. Nor do they understand how cognition, affect, and motivation work together in learning or how others help them learn. Even those who facilitate mediated learning experiences—parents, teachers, and others—do not know when or how mediated learning takes place.

But true learning success depends on the degree to which individuals know how to learn. And learning how to learn depends on the quality of social interactions, which assist and promote learning, flexibility in thinking, and human competency. Cognitive Enrichment Advantage (CEA) teachers help students with human competency—intelligence as it refers to one's ability to function well in the world—by mediating metastrategic knowledge students can use to build strategies that help them function more competently and understand what it means to be an effective independent and interdependent, lifelong learner.

Increasing evidence demonstrates that mediated learning theory provides the framework for powerful teaching methods, such as CEA, that can support inquiry learning and truly maximize students' learning potential. CEA offers an effective and comprehensive approach for combining mediated and inquiry learning. Inquiry learning means to learn by exploring, accommodating, and assimilating stimuli to which one is directly exposed. Examples of inquiry learning include students creating then conducting a science experiment or writing a research report exploring a question they posed themselves. It is the most common kind of learning according to Piaget and Feuerstein. Inquiry learning depends on mediated learning, a type of social construction of knowledge. Only through mediated learning do students acquire enough learning-to-learn competency to do well with inquiry learning.

Messing about to Construct Knowledge

Six-year-old Willard ran into the room. "I know how it works!" he cried. The diagnostician working with Willard to determine why the boy was having so much trouble learning asked him to explain. Willard described his serendipitous experience: "I know how you write the numbers 10 to 20! See, first you write '1' for each number and then you write '1,' '2,' '3,' . . . beside each of the 1s." He was glowing from his hard-won insight. To be sure, this insight was based on his own informal knowledge rather than a formal method shared by his teacher. Willard had been "messing about" (Hawkins 1974) with the formal knowledge symbols for numbers that were giving him so much trouble in the classroom. His teacher's careful sharing of the textbook knowledge had not brought this insight. Organizing and building his own model had. Hawkins describes learning as "an ongoing process of

reorganizing and testing, through which new knowledge and new plans may modify our behavior" (18). In Piagetian terms, learning also depends on the internal processes of constructing knowledge through interaction with these stimuli (Piaget 1976).

Research on how students (and all learners) construct knowledge demonstrates that the internal processes involve much more than replacing old facts with new ones. Hawkins points out that humans can store vast amounts of knowledge in memory, but only if they can connect that knowledge in a meaningful way with their personal worldviews regarding how to go about learning. If not, very little of that knowledge may be stored at all and even less of it is available for relevant future use.

Inquiry Learning

Today, many schools provide more time for student-centered, active, inquiry learning activities that allow learners to choose open-ended activities, engage in critical thinking, investigate the natural world, and test personal "theories" (Hawkins 1974; Weir 1989). As a result, students have the opportunity to accomplish the internal processing that is crucial to learning. To achieve successful inquiry learning, however, students need to develop effective, independent learning skills (see Figure 2.1).

FIGURE 2.1

Successful Inquiry Learning

Weir (1989) discusses several prerequisites to student success in inquiry learning activities. Student success in inquiry learning activities requires the ability to

1. become aware of personal goals,

2. see formal school knowledge as relevant to one's personal goals,

3. reflect on cognitive strategies,

4. reflect on the underlying structure of given knowledge, and

5. understand the significance and implications of what one has learned.

Many students are not explicitly helped to develop effective, independent learning skills, and, hence, are often described as passive learners (Feuerstein et al. 1980). These learners are not limited to those with lower intelligence test scores (Greenberg, Coleman, and Rankin 1993). Even some students classified as intellectually gifted can display a lack of explicit knowledge of how to engage in effective critical thinking and overcome challenges they face in learning. For these passive students, the trial and error of messing about frequently does not result in progress toward a workable theory of what learners need to know to proceed in the task. In fact, these students display little purposeful behavior in approaching the learning experience and engaging in a process that leads to accomplishing a goal. These students often become bored and acquire little meaningful pragmatic knowledge that they can connect to formal knowledge, even when learning activities are well designed to encourage critical thinking. Passive learners often do not receive the help that would allow them to overcome their learning problems because too few educators have the explicit knowledge about cognitive education that they need to help students become active, independent learners.

Theories of Learning

The framework of the CEA teaching method is derived in large part from Reuven Feuerstein's theory of mediated learning experience (Feuerstein et al. 1980). It also incorporates the theoretical work of Lev Vygotsky (1978) and Jean Piaget (1976) as well as research related to the following: community influence on intellectual development (Heath 1983), nurturing active learning and effective small-group use of computers (Weir 1989), effective transfer of knowledge and skills (Perkins and Salomin 1989), engaging students in cooperative learning activities and social skills development (Kagan 1992), collaborative learning with people of all ages (Shotter 1993), and effective organizational learning (learning by those within the organization that leads to successful operation and fulfillment of a shared vision) that impacts attempts to establish a school-based community of learners (Fullan 1993; Hargrove 1995, 1998; Maurer 1996; Senge 1993; and Senge et al. 1999).

Vygotsky's Zone of Proximal Development

According to Vygotsky (1978), "cognitive change comes from the transformation of knowledge among persons . . . into knowledge within a person. . . . "(57). Cognitive change occurs only when a more knowledgeable other helps a learner move as far as he can with assistance beyond the place where the learner could no longer solve problems independently. As a result, cognitive growth emerges in what Vygotsky terms the *zone of proximal development*.

But how does the more knowledgeable person help the learner in the zone of proximal development? Brofenbrenner (1991) and Hundeide (1991) describe evidence that reciprocity is crucial to cognitive growth, that human competence and character require a strong feedback loop between the developing person and the one providing assistance. In addition, reciprocal activities are effective only if they

take place regularly over extended periods and exhibit progressively more complex forms (Brofenbrenner). Research findings such as these are helpful, but they do not explain the qualities of an effective mediator in such learning experiences. Feuerstein provides the most comprehensive description of what takes place during a mediated learning experience (Feuerstein et al. 1980). This theory describes the qualities of the interaction within the zone of proximal development.

Mediating Learning Experiences

Feuerstein's theory of mediated learning experience is a social constructivist view of learning in that it describes how individuals construct a meaningful world through the reciprocal interactions they have with more knowledgeable others who share a system of cultural meanings and values (Feuerstein et al. 1980; Feuerstein, Klein, and Tannenbaum 1990).

Feuerstein reports that mediated learning occurs when a more knowledgeable person prompts a less knowledgeable person to label, compare, categorize, and give meaning to a present experience as it relates to prior and future ones (Feuerstein et al. 1980). As learners relate their personal knowledge to ideas expressed or elicited by the mediator, they make advances in learning that eventually move the zone of proximal development to a higher level. With exposure to high quality mediated learning experiences, learners develop a flexibility of thinking and learning and an increasing need for learning at more complex levels. One can engage in mediated learning interactions—as either mediator or recipient—at any age.

Influence of Culture on Mediated Learning

Mediated learning occurs naturally in many interactions between parent and child and between teacher and student because of the older individual's need to transmit cultural knowledge to the younger generation. According to Feuerstein, humans manifest characteristics of mediators of learning experiences spontaneously in their interactions with those whom they nurture due to an instinctive and deep need to transmit their culture (Feuerstein et al. 1980). Indigenous peoples living near the Arctic teach their children about the different types of snow and how to survive in extremely cold temperatures. People from desert cultures teach their children about the different kinds of sand and how to survive where water is not plentiful. These ethnic groups think and learn as effectively as any other ethnic group. They can solve many problems within their environment, make judgments, and reason equally well. Their ability to learn within their own environments is quite similar. But what each culture knows about the world differs significantly.

A mismatch can result between the learner and the teacher-mediator when mediated learning that occurs in the home or local community is based on values different from those at school. For example, a student may learn at home that it is wrong to question anyone in authority, then this student is expected to question and perhaps even challenge the teacher at school. This student does not respond as teachers expect. Heath offers the example of teachers asking students to make up stories, but some of their students had learned at home that making up stories is lying (1983). When conflicts between school and home exist, learners may withdraw from one or both worlds. Alienation often occurs, resulting at times in a lack of academic achievement similar to that of learners with disabilities. Feuerstein reports observations of adolescents who had grown up under stressful conditions where caregivers were unable to transmit their culture freely through mediated learning (Feuerstein et al. 1980). These adolescents displayed many and frequently severe cognitive deficiencies and other affective and motivational problems similar to individuals with disabling conditions. In other situations, family members who lose touch with their own cultural values also lose the intrinsic motivation to provide high quality mediated learning. For example, immigrant parents who want their children to learn the culture and language of their adopted country may withhold their own culture from their children, encouraging them to learn from their teachers and not from themselves.

In addition to cultural alienation, other factors such as poverty, family disruption, and disabilities can place individuals at risk for learning how to learn and mask potential capabilities (Greenberg, Coleman, and Rankin 1993). CEA teachers facilitate mediated learning experiences in the classroom to prevent or overcome these learning problems; therefore, learning potential is maximized in schools using CEA or similar teaching methods based on Feuerstein's theory (Feuerstein et al. 1980).

The Art and Science of Mediated Learning

Mediators display the art of mediated learning by using implicit knowledge to make decisions about how to mediate, decisions that may involve good judgment and insight they cannot explain. But armed with explicit knowledge of mediated learning experience theory, mediators can develop the science of mediated learning and become mindful of specific qualities of mediated learning, carefully consider their intent within the learning experience, and systematically plan ways to use mediated learning to facilitate the learner's ability to overcome cognitive, affective, and motivational difficulties. To provide high quality mediated learning experiences, teachers must develop both art and science skills. The explicit "rules" that make up the science of being a mediator only provide the steps to the dance. Every mediator must draw on the art of mediated learning to dance well with the learner. The art is necessary because no two dancers are the same even if they use the same general steps. The art of mediated learning allows mediators to manifest an intuitive, reciprocal relationship with the learner, while the science enables them to consider

clearly the explicit knowledge that is critically important in the process of mediating learning experiences.

To understand the art and science of mediating learning experiences, it helps to focus first on the kinds of problems learners face when constructing knowledge for themselves. For example, individuals may have difficulty relating objects and events to prior knowledge, they may find their prior knowledge incompatible with the new information, or they may "learn" something that will not help them become effective learners within their society. Fortunately, others can help learners overcome these problems by means of mediating learning experiences. As long as the mediator and student share a common cultural understanding, and the student's social, economic, health, and safety needs are met, the student will most likely receive sufficient mediated learning to become reasonably successful in learning situations.

The most common initial reaction CEA consultants receive when describing mediated learning to teachers is the following: "What's so different about that? Isn't mediated learning just good teaching and good parenting?" The answer could be yes only if the world shared one common culture and excellent social and health conditions, and learning difficulties did not occur. Because the world is a place where cultural alienation and poor social and health conditions are an everyday problem, society continually faces situations where good teaching, good parenting, and the spontaneously manifested art of mediated learning are not enough—even if their occurrence could be guaranteed. Therefore, it is important to become a teacher-mediator who is aware of the art of mediated learning and knowledgeable about the science of mediating learning experiences. Helping teachers become teacher-mediators is a primary goal of this handbook.

According to Feuerstein, the mediator intentionally takes control of some stimuli in the environment and makes changes so the learner focuses on these specific stimuli (Feuerstein et al. 1980). The mediator also intentionally helps the learner respond in effective ways to the stimuli.

The mediator selects and organizes the stimuli for the learner as influenced by his interaction with the learner and the context of the learning experience. Some of the stimuli and the structures, or schemas, they integrate with inside the mind of the learner also change as the learner forms new relationships among the bits of information and other information already stored in the brain. Some of the changes, but certainly not all, are influenced by the mediator. The mediator once again comes between the learner and some of his or her responses, maintaining the mediated learning experience beyond the phases of input of information and integration to include the expression of a response.

Mediated learning takes place, according to Feuerstein, only when the mediator displays the following qualities: intent, or catching and focusing attention; meaning, or energizing awareness and making the experience personally relevant; transcendence, or going beyond the immediate needs to make a decontextualized connection between ideas and their use in other contexts; and reciprocity, or engaging the learner by establishing a positive connection of acceptance, trust, and understanding between them (Feuerstein et al. 1980).

Cognitive Deficiencies and Parameters of Mediated Learning

Feuerstein writes extensively about cognitive deficiencies. He also identifies parameters of mediated learning. This handbook outlines the adaptation of both the deficiencies and the parameters in CEA. The cognitive deficiencies have been combined into twelve Building Blocks of Thinking and include a shared vocabulary for cognitive processes that foster effective thinking when approaching learning experiences, making meaning of learning experiences, and confirming learning experiences. The parameters of mediated learning are called Tools of Learning in CEA, and they focus on understanding feelings and motivating behavior in ways that foster independent and interdependent learning. A thorough discussion of the Building Blocks and Tools appears in Chapter 3.

The Impact of High and Low Quality Mediated Learning

A learner exposed to high quality mediated learning experiences over an extended period develops an increased capacity to anticipate relationships between objects and events in the environment. As Feuerstein states, the learner develops "approaches to mentally organizing, manipulating, and acting on information [gathered from memory as well as new sources]" (Feuerstein et al. 1980, 16). As a result, the learner becomes an active participant in learning. If, however, the learner does not receive an adequate amount of high quality mediated learning experiences, serious learning problems can result. See Figure 2.2 for a description of the impact of high quality and low quality mediated learning.

The mediated learning method helps teacher-mediators achieve three basic goals in the classroom:

1. to create a laboratory for learning in the classroom by developing learning activities that are personally and culturally relevant to students, facilitate active involvement, foster collaborative learning, focus student attention on the process as well as the product of learning, and offer complex problem-solving opportunities

2. to serve as a mediator of learning experiences in teacher-student interactions, striving to help each student move beyond his or her present level of development through effective use of principles of mediated learning and CEA teaching practices

3. to help students develop self-regulated behavior, a propensity for lifelong learning, and the ability to adapt the twelve Building Blocks of Thinking

FIGURE 2.2

Impact of High and Low Quality Mediated Learning

With a sufficient degree of high quality mediated learning, learners

❑ develop the ability and desire to adapt to new situations,

❑ learn how to learn,

❑ transfer what they learn from one situation to others, and

❑ become active generators of information.

Without a sufficient degree of high quality of mediated learning, learners

❑ develop bad habits for learning such as ineffective use of the Building Blocks and Tools,

❑ transfer very little of what they learn from one situation to others,

❑ display limited motivation to learn independently, and

❑ become passive recipients of information.

(cognitive processes that foster effective thinking) and eight Tools of Learning (affective-motivational approaches that foster independent and interdependent learning) into personal learning strategies for use in real-life and classroom situations.

The ABCs of Becoming a Teacher-Mediator

This section describes the role of the teacher-mediator and techniques for facilitating high quality mediated learning experiences. *The Cognitive Enrichment Advantage Family-School Partnership Handbook* focuses on the role of parents and other family members as mediators.

Essential Qualities of Effective Mediators

Four qualities must be present for mediated learning to occur: reciprocity, intent, meaning, and transcendence (adapted from Feuerstein et al. 1980). Effective teacher-mediators add additional qualities based on the needs of the learner (see Figure 2.3).

FIGURE 2.3

Essential Qualities of Effective Mediators

For a high quality mediated learning experience to occur, mediators need to display four essential qualities when interacting with learners:

1. Reciprocity: establishing a positive connection of acceptance, trust, and understanding

2. Intent: catching and focusing attention

3. Meaning: energizing awareness and making the experience personally relevant

4. Transcendence: expanding understanding beyond the current learning context

---

Reciprocity

Reciprocity is establishing a positive connection of acceptance, trust, and understanding between learner and mediator. Reciprocity is necessary before the remaining three qualities, intent, meaning, and transcendence, can exist effectively. Hundeide (1991) states that it is important to establish a positive connection between mediator and learner through display of affection and mutual expression of acceptance, trust, and empathy. CEA teacher-mediators fine-tune interactions based on the learner's behavior.

An analogy for reciprocity is jazz improvisation. The musicians listen carefully to each other, playing off the others' musical message, alternately assuming the lead role. In the classroom, reciprocity helps teacher-mediators continuously assess the learning experience to make needed changes to ensure activities challenge learners in a positive way and learners are within their zones of proximal development. In other words, teacher-mediators continuously adjust learning activities, or facilitate adjustments made by the students themselves, so activities are neither too easy nor too difficult but clearly challenging. As a result, teacher-mediators facilitate mediated learning experiences when and where learners express a need for them or when teachers identify the need to make adjustments.

Intent

The quality of intent, catching and focusing attention, within a mediated learning experience refers to the teacher's preparedness—the teacher-mediator should be well organized and have thought about how to catch and focus attention in advance of the learning experience. But the intent often needs to change during the activity. As important as it is for teacher-mediators to have intent to implement

specific objectives within learning activities, it is equally important that learners feel ownership of intent within mediated learning experiences. For example, the teacher might plan to focus attention on developing a precise understanding of a paragraph. During the lesson, she allows students enough freedom to lead the group into exploring the definition of a sentence. The teacher observes that the students do not have a precise understanding of a sentence and changes her intent based on that observation to teach sentences instead of paragraphs.

Intent must be in sync with reciprocity. This means that teacher-mediators facilitate the construction of a clear intent with each learner by asking questions and responding to cues, sometimes leading the other musicians in their musical collaboration and sometimes following. When teacher-mediators believe that one or more learners are sufficiently challenged (in their zones of proximal development) to warrant a mediated learning experience, they ask questions that focus attention on some shared intent.

To include intent and reciprocity in mediated learning experiences, teacher-mediators can engage in one or more of the following behaviors:

1. Select activities and schedule the presentation of concepts and objects that assist learners in reaching the intended goal, while maintaining a positive connection with learners. In other words, teachers are responsive to cues from learners, and there is trust and empathy.

   Example: The teacher-mediator, in a positive and supportive manner, points out a math problem that a student has computed incorrectly. He asks the student to explain the process the student used to work the problem by showing the teacher each step in the order the student worked.

2. State intent to learners while monitoring students' willingness to participate and adjusting the interaction based on this feedback.

   Example: The teacher-mediator says to a learner, "I want to help you edit the report you wrote. What do you think? Are you satisfied with your report as it stands? No? How would you like to edit the report? Would you rather edit the report by yourself? OK, you edit it by yourself, then we will talk about it."

Intent sometimes involves changing objects or events, the learner, or the teacher-mediator, making reciprocity integral to intent. Teacher-mediators are responsible for attending to the student's cues and maintaining a positive effect. Only in this manner do they establish an authentic intent with learners and ensure a better opportunity for students to respond to the mediated learning experience. Examples of helpful questions to establish intent include the following:

❑ "What is important for us to pay attention to in this activity?"

❑ "What are we trying to do?"

❑ "What do you know at this time about this activity?"

❑ "What would you like to know about this subject that you don't already know?"

Meaning

Meaning is energizing awareness and making the experience personally relevant. The quality of meaning within a mediated learning experience is effective only if it is personally relevant to each individual learner. Through reciprocity, mediators make sure that learners accept and share the meaning. Feuerstein states that mediators express meaning through affective behavior that lends power to the interaction: sharing or displaying excitement, enthusiasm, and caring (Feuerstein et al. 1980). Teacher-mediators find what is significant to learners and use this to fuel the interaction.

Meaning addresses cognitive, affective, and motivational needs of the learner: cognitive meaning is objective ("That is a famous painting."); affective meaning is subjective ("I love that painting."); and motivational meaning addresses reasons for action ("I will be able to become a better painter if I understand the driving force behind Picasso's works.") Sometimes only one of the three aspects is the focus of the mediated learning experience, at other times all three are. The idea is to find value within the learning experience that provides a sense of wonder and joy—even fear and anxiety—in learning and to explore the "whys" of learning. Exploring learners' assumptions underlying a learning experience is a powerful way to establish the quality of meaning. As with intent, teacher-mediators facilitate meaning by paying attention to cues from learners and asking questions.

To include meaning in mediated learning experiences, CEA teacher-mediators engage in one or more of the following behaviors:

1. Share with learners a personal interest and emotional involvement in the activity.

   Example: Teacher-mediator says to learner, "I can't wait to go on our nature hike! I just love to see the brightly colored leaves on the trees this time of year."

2. Discuss the importance of the activity with learners.

   Example: Teacher-mediator says to learner, "You will feel so good about yourself when you learn to read. I can still remember when I learned how to read. This is really a special time."

3. Share an objective or subjective value.

    Example: Teacher-mediator says to learner, "I feel really uncomfortable when I hear that kind of language. I don't want you to use it around me."

Examples of helpful questions and comments to facilitate the quality of meaning within a mediated learning experience include the following:

❏ "Why is this topic/idea important?"

❏ "You say that because. . . . ?"

❏ "What makes you so anxious about doing this activity?"

❏ "You are really eager to get started with this project. Why is that?"

Transcendence

Transcendence is expanding understanding beyond the current learning context. The quality of transcendence within a mediated learning experience is very important because it helps learners become active generators of information who can apply what they learn outside of the current context. By means of transcendence, learners decontextualize some aspect of the learning experience and make connections to past and future situations, expanding their understanding. Transcendence helps learners build flexibility of thinking because they gain an understanding of the framework underlying some concept or the process of learning that can help them learn better. They build the knowledge needed to develop personal learning strategies in any kind of situation and explore relationships at a useful and deep level between some aspect of the given learning experience and other experiences.

Teacher-mediators draw on reciprocity, intent, and meaning to ensure transcendence occurs. For effective transcendence, teacher-mediators must help learners go beyond the immediate context to make a decontextualized connection to many other contexts in prior and future situations. For example, if a learner is anxious about a math assignment because he thinks he is no good at arithmetic, the teacher-mediator might help the learner transcend the anxiety by facilitating the learner's understanding of anxiety and how it interferes with learning in this and other situations. Then the teacher-mediator can help the student summarize this understanding in a principle about the effect of negative emotions on learning in any situation such as "If I gain control over my anxiety about failing in a learning experience, then I will be able to learn more effectively."

Transcendence is a form of bridging, a technique for transferring knowledge from one learning situation to another (see chapter 4 for a complete discussion of bridging and transfer). Transcendence often involves a focus on the process of learning in a generalized or decontextualized sense rather than a focus on the product of the given learning experience. In the example above, the focus on anxiety and its effect on learning is a focus on the process of learning. When teacher-mediators help students gain insight into the need for specific Building Blocks of Thinking and Tools of Learning, a high level of transcendence can occur.

To include transcendence in a mediated learning experience, CEA teacher-mediators engage in one or more of the following behaviors:

1. Help learners reflect on some process connected to the activity.

    Example: Teacher-mediator says to learner, "Let's think together about how the artist drew the bumblebee. Why do you suppose she drew those lines in that way? What do you want to say about bumblebees with the lines you draw?"

2. Help learners understand how the activity (or parts of it) or their approach to the activity relates to other activities (or parts of this activity).

    Example: Teacher-mediator says to learner, "What are you learning as you do these subtraction problems that relates to the kind of subtraction problems we learned about last week?"

3. Help learners think about a principle that applies to this activity as well as many other situations.

    Example: Teacher-mediator discusses with learners the need for respect in getting along with others at school, at home, and in the world in general.

Examples of helpful questions for effective transcendence within a learning experience include the following:

❑ "How is your anxiety in this situation similar to what you felt during the math project last week? What can you learn from this experience that can help you in the future?"

❑ "What does this insect have in common with other insects? with spiders? with birds? How are you making these comparisons? Can you compare other living things using the same process? Help me write a principle about making comparisons. If I make comparisons by _____, then I will be able to learn better."

Additional Tips for Mediating Learning Experiences

❑ Many mediated learning experiences can occur within one classroom activity. Some might occur with a group of students; others might focus on one student's needs.

❏ Mediated learning experiences are most effective when they occur within a student's zone of proximal development, where learners feel clearly the need for mediation.

❏ Mediated learning experiences are of higher quality when the mediator elicits ideas from learners. In fact, mediated learning may not affect learners when the mediator transmits ideas to learners, particularly when those ideas are not personally relevant to them.

❏ It is important for teacher-mediators to learn to ask questions that help learners play an active role in the mediated learning experience.

❏ A powerful learning environment exists when all members of the class become mediators for others.

Creating a Laboratory for Learning in the Classroom

Perhaps the clearest metaphor for using a mediated learning teaching method is to picture the classroom as a laboratory for learning: a place where people enjoy challenges, class members test the validity of their beliefs about the way the world works, the learning community places great value on every class member's developing an understanding of the process of learning, and the classroom atmosphere enhances the possibilities for high quality mediated learning experiences. Figure 2.4 describes characteristics of a classroom that is a laboratory for learning.

Learning School

Before establishing a laboratory for learning in the classroom, class members must possess a shared understanding of the expectations for learning within the classroom. Many classrooms comprise students from highly diverse backgrounds, personal worldviews, and cultures. Students need to "learn school," in other words, understand what the school and teachers expect of them and overcome the confusion that invariably results when students enter the classroom with widely varying understanding of school expectations.

First, it is important that school staff and family members share an understanding of the purpose for school. Teachers must explore family views about the purpose of school and expectations for learning. When school staff members truly understand the personal views of the families they serve, they can work with family members to address discrepancies. This kind of collaboration can overcome negative stereotyping that commonly occurs when school staff and families do not share a purpose for schools.

In addition, to become a lifelong learner, students need to understand that learning occurs in all kinds of situations and in all kinds of places in and out of

FIGURE 2.4

Characteristics of a Laboratory for Learning Classroom

In a laboratory for learning

- ❏ The learning community values the process of learning as much as the product.

- ❏ The learning community understands that success and failure depend on the process of learning used.

- ❏ The learning community sees or considers problems as natural learning opportunities.

- ❏ The learning community expects to find solutions to problems that occur.

- ❏ Students construct knowledge with the help of other members of the learning community in mediated learning experiences.

- ❏ Students can find connections between school learning and the world outside school.

- ❏ Students can connect personal experience to the formal knowledge of school.

- ❏ The learning community expects everyone to learn.

- ❏ The learning community encourages individual differences in approaching learning.

- ❏ The learning community values collaborative learning as a means of enhancing the social construction of knowledge by individuals and groups.

school. Family-school partnerships are very important in building this understanding. When family members and teachers share a metastrategic vocabulary, family members help students focus on the process of learning outside of school just as teachers do in the classroom. The partnerships also provide the opportunity for a more subtle and critically important outcome: understanding differences between home and school expectations for learning and subsequently changing these expectations if necessary. For example, the teacher can change classroom expectations to be more consistent with what students learned from their parents, or, more commonly, parents can help their children learn about the school's expectations and how they differ from the expectations of family and culture. All these expectations exert a powerful influence on young people.

A study published in the early 1980s still receives a great deal of attention because of its findings concerning cultural expectations for learning in and outside of school. Shirley Brice Heath (1983) describes the many differences between school learning and learning at home in three different cultural settings based on her ethnographic study of language development. Her work is particularly valuable because it highlights the vast differences in assumptions that students bring into

the classroom about the use of language and how one is expected to learn. Heath concludes that teachers must understand their own expectations for learning as well as the values that students bring into the classroom, then they can help students learn school more appropriately and effectively.

For example, in Heath's study one group of children had learned in their homes that adults teach them one "right" way to use language. These children were confused when teachers asked them to write new endings to fiction stories. They considered this lying. Another group of children had learned in their homes to change language in every situation. Their teachers viewed them as not trustworthy or as having poor memories because these students felt free to change stories about events that had actually taken place.

By learning school, CEA students develop a shared understanding of the assumptions and beliefs that are a part of a laboratory for learning. In any school, it is important that students learn school by understanding teacher expectations. In CEA schools, it is important that students and family members who are partners with the school also understand teacher expectations regarding the classroom as a laboratory for learning. Figure 2.5 presents four aspects of school activities that students must understand if they are to learn school and participate successfully in oral and written activities.

FIGURE 2.5

Four Aspects of Learning School

To learn school, students need to understand teacher expectations for the following:

❑ where to do what

❑ when to do what

❑ how to work with small parts of subject content in isolation, such as lessons that focus on vowel sounds needed for reading or math facts needed for algebra

❑ how to be a student, how to learn in the school environment. In CEA schools, this statement means to be collaborative, to experiment, to learn how to learn. In some other schools, it means to be quiet, memorize what the teacher lectures about, and respond with one right answer.

Methods for helping students learn school must not devalue the culture or personal worldview of the student's family or community. Indeed, teachers need to evaluate the expectations for learning carefully; they should not assume that school values should have priority over family values. It is very important to ensure that all students can join the "club" of school (Smith 1986). Only then can students appropriately apply whatever they already know about the world outside of school to learning in school. By joining the club of school, Smith means that students understand and act on the expectations of membership that let them know that it is OK or not OK to share and connect their personal theories and knowledge as they learn formal knowledge in school. Teacher-mediators who use the art and science of mediated learning in the classroom can help overcome disparate expectations of school and learning.

Students with expectations that are different from those of the school—for example, expectations that they should be seen and not heard, that they should not look directly at the teacher, that they should not make their needs known—are often considered poor learners, unmotivated, or resistant. In reality, these students may be dealing with implicit and conflicting values (in home and school) that they do not fully understand. Classrooms that make these implicit values explicit can greatly enhance learning.

Mediated Learning and Good Teaching

Many good teachers use mediated learning methods without an explicit and deliberate focus on them and without discerning how they mediated. (CEA's intent is to provide teachers with explicit knowledge regarding the use of mediated learning in the classroom.) A look at the subtle differences between good teaching and CEA's mediated learning teaching method appears in Figure 2.6.

CEA mediated learning teaching methods vary in subtle yet significant ways from other mediated learning instructional methods. A number of researchers have developed "scaffolded instructional methods" as described by Ashman and Conway (1997). Scaffolded instructional methods are associated with interpretations of Vygotsky's work on social interactions within learners' zones of proximal development where "learning is mediated by an expert guiding a novice through a task to ensure that the learner acquires the expert's skills" (Ashman and Conway 1997, 137).

Scaffolded instructional methods share a similar goal with other approaches based on Feuerstein's theory (Feuerstein et al. 1980): helping students learn more effectively at an independent level. They focus student attention on the process of learning and the need for self-evaluation. Scaffolding, however, teaches specific strategies developed by experts. In contrast, CEA, like other Feuerstein approaches, teaches students how to develop their own strategies based on general metastrategic knowledge. This knowledge is contained in the Building Blocks of Thinking and the Tools of Independent Learning as chapter 3 describes. Scaffolding also tends to limit the focus to approaching the specific subject matter tasks. CEA and other Feuerstein approaches seek to expand focus beyond the immediate needs of the

FIGURE 2.6

Mediated Learning Is More than Good Teaching

1. Good teachers teach students what they need to know. Teacher-mediators collaborate as another learner with students to reflect on what each person already knows and to see how this knowledge connects to something new.

2. Good teachers often focus students' attention on tne lesson content. Teacher-mediators also clarify and expand students' understanding beyond the immediate needs of the content and context.

3. Good teachers often isolate specific concepts for teaching. Teacher-mediators also connect concepts to students' real-world experiences.

4. Good teachers provide students with opportunities to produce right answers based on given information. Teacher-mediators more frequently provide opportunities for students to explore ideas, seek relevant information, and construct meaning independently and collaboratively.

5. Good teachers lead students through learning experiences as a part of a carefully selected curriculum. Teacher-mediators also adapt activities so they are personally relevant and challenging.

6. Good teachers often model tasks, break tasks into smaller parts, and reteach when necessary. Teacher-mediators help students learn to construct their own learning strategies to solve problems.

7. Good teachers make certain to share the right answer with students. Teacher-mediators also provide extra time and assistance so every student can reflect on the process of reaching the right answer and find an approach that leads to an effective response.

8. Good teachers usually provide students with feedback related to their learning products and often reward students based on teacher standards. Teacher-mediators also encourage students to evaluate the individual process they used that led to a product and provide feedback and encouragement (rather than rewards) related to the process of learning based on mutually determined standards.

9. Good teachers often lead class discussions in which they ask questions and students respond. Teacher-mediators more frequently empower students to ask questions and to share insights with the group.

10. Good teachers establish an atmosphere in which students feel successful when they can learn easily and share what they know. Teacher-mediators establish an atmosphere that measures success by how much one is willing to accept challenges and learn how to learn.

subject matter to learning of any content in any setting. In fact, mediated learning experiences are not considered successful unless such transcendence occurs.

Employing the art and science of mediated learning methods requires a focus on a number of aspects of teaching and learning, including the qualities of an effective teacher-mediator, the classroom setting, curriculum content, and learning activities. Because communities, school districts, and national values determine curriculum content, *The Cognitive Enrichment Advantage Teacher Handbook* does not address it in detail. Curriculum content that goes beyond the acquisition of factual information and focuses on development of student insight into various ways of exploring knowledge in subject matter domains is more compatible with mediated learning approaches.

Establishing an Open Classroom Atmosphere

An open classroom atmosphere is critically important for maximizing learning potential and enhancing mediated learning. When students feel accepted, safe, and challenged, they more readily enter their zones of proximal development. They more readily seek mediated learning experiences.

In an open classroom atmosphere, standards are high for all members of the learning community. Everyone is expected to work toward becoming an effective independent and interdependent learner, capable of striving for excellence. In a closed classroom atmosphere where the classroom is usually a stage for producing right answers, the focus is on the products of learning. Paradoxically, this product-oriented focus does not lead to excellence for all students. Instead, the culture of the classroom values what students already know and can share in a final form. Attention to how to learn gets pushed aside.

In an open classroom, the primary focus is on the learning process and how to improve one's approach to learning experiences. In this laboratory for learning, students become aware of the many personal learning strategies they can develop for themselves based on the Building Blocks of Thinking and Tools of Learning. Right answers are examples of effective thinking and learning; yet, most learning is directed toward more complex ideas where the one right answer is not always relevant. Figure 2.7 compares a closed and open classroom atmosphere.

Co-opting

Co-opting takes the learning opportunity away from the student. It occurs when a student responds inadequately and the teacher does not give her the opportunity or assistance necessary to solve the existing problem herself. For example, if a teacher calls on one student who provides an inadequate response and then immediately focuses attention on another student who can provide a better response, that teacher has co-opted. Co-opting also occurs when students receive instructions on how to approach a project without an opportunity to develop their own approach to the learning experience.

When a student gives an inadequate response in a laboratory for learning, everyone works together to understand the learning process and how this student might solve the problem. The student is given time to plan an approach to the learning experience based on a Building Block or Tool. She has the opportunity to derive a more adequate response rather than having her responses co-opted by others.

In many classrooms that are not laboratories for learning, some students inevitably "fall between the cracks," providing inadequate answers when they are forced to share and contributing little insight into the learning experience. Teachers and other students co-opt their learning opportunities. In a laboratory for learning, however, these students receive the support they need to overcome their cognitive,

FIGURE 2.7

Characteristics of Open and Closed Classroom Atmosphere

Standards held by members of an open classroom atmosphere that enhances mediated learning:

❑ Members expect all students to learn.

❑ Members respect all students for their efforts to learn.

❑ Members encourage thinking that leads to effective learning.

❑ Members support learning opportunities (no co-opting).*

❑ Members value the process of learning as least as much as the product.

❑ Members honor effective, independent and interdependent, lifelong learning.

❑ Members treat the classroom as a laboratory for learning, not a stage for producing right answers.

Impact of a closed classroom atmosphere where the classroom is a stage for producing right answers:

❑ Students feel lucky when their performance is satisfactory and unlucky when it is not.

❑ Students are not motivated to participate in mediated learning.

❑ Students feel no need to learn how to learn.

❑ Students' learning opportunities are often co-opted* by others in the classroom.

*To co-opt is to deprive a student of a learning opportunity by means of providing responses for the student that eliminate any need for the student to seek an adequate response himself.

---

affective, and motivational problems. Therefore, they can be expected to contribute good thinking and insight to class activities.

Students who are frequently co-opted often stop paying attention to class interactions and do not participate actively in learning experiences. Many of these students become afraid to respond in front of others. In contrast, when classrooms are laboratories for learning, students learn to feel safe and to trust others enough to seek help openly. Students come to feel comfortable experimenting with their learning. They learn over time that class members help each other find approaches to solving problems.

Successful establishment of a laboratory for learning in the classroom requires the support of all class members. Teachers cannot and should not be the only class member who functions as a mediator. Facilitating the social construction of knowledge and avoiding co-opting becomes the responsibility of all class members. Many teacher-mediators find over time that class members enjoy the challenge of solving problems and feel good when other class members overcome learning difficulties and move through their zones of proximal development.

At times a teacher must co-opt so as not to lose the flow of the lesson as well as the attention of the rest of the students. For example, when explaining how condensation occurs on a glass filled with ice water, the teacher may have to co-opt a student's inadequate response to make the process clear to everyone and not make them wait until the student finds a strategy that will help her share a more accurate response. There are also times when a student is unwilling to plan or attempt a new approach, or no one is able to provide the support necessary for the student to succeed in the present situation.

Activities in a Laboratory for Learning

CEA teacher-mediators find that students are able to engage in increasingly more challenging activities in a laboratory for learning. Routine kinds of activities do not allow students to use fully the power they gain as they develop learning strategies based on the Building Blocks and Tools, nor do they move students into the zone of proximal development where mediated learning experiences best take place. Challenging and open-ended activities that might have caused frustration and acting out behavior in the past now provide excitement and joy in learning for many students.

Not all activities are appropriate for use in a laboratory for learning. Often, curriculum materials possess some but not all of the critical attributes described in Figure 2.8. But teachers can adapt most activities to meet the critical attributes better and maximize learning potential. Some teacher-mediators use the critical attributes to assist them in making decisions about the purchase of new educational materials. They have been especially helpful in evaluating educational software. The market is full of educational software that looks very clever and exciting on the surface but is actually of little value in furthering student active involvement in the learning process.

Using activities that enhance the classroom as a laboratory for learning, establishing an open atmosphere where collaborative and cooperative learning can take place, and building a shared vocabulary of metastrategic knowledge students can use to build personal learning strategies is only the beginning. Students must have the ability to transfer what they learn to the real world as well as to other classroom settings. Chapter 3 discusses the shared vocabulary of metastrategic knowledge, and chapter 4 guides teachers in using this metastrategic knowledge to facilitate transfer.

FIGURE 2.8

Critical Attributes for Activities in a Laboratory for Learning

When evaluating activities to determine whether they meet the standard for a classroom laboratory for learning, teachers can consider the following critical attributes.

1. These activities require students to integrate ideas and share the results of careful thinking. They do not rely merely on recall of specific, unconnected facts.

2. These activities encourage students to participate actively even when others are speaking by evaluating others' responses and helping others solve problems. They do not allow students to sit passively and wait on others to have their turns or take over (co-opt) others' learning.

3. These activities allow students to make choices about what they will do on some parts of many activities. They do not require all students to do exactly the same tasks in every case.

4. These activities include some tasks for which there is no one best response. They do not require students to "read the teacher's mind."

5. These activities help students connect isolated skills to their need in real-life activities. They do not present drill and practice tasks without showing how they are used with other skills in real-life activities.

6. These activities focus students' attention on process as much as or more than product—on improving their approach to the learning experience. They do not focus students' attention exclusively on producing right answers.

7. These activities assist teachers in observing how students process information as they perform. They do not result in documenting only the product of each student's thinking.

8. These activities focus students' attention on the need for Self-Regulation, a CEA Tool of Learning (see chapter 3). They do not always regulate behavior for students.

9. These activities provide enough challenge for students so they can build a Feeling of Competence, a CEA Tool of Learning (see chapter 3). They are neither boring nor too difficult.

10. These activities transcend the actual skills involved by providing insight that goes beyond the immediate needs of the task. They are not limited to focus on the present situation.

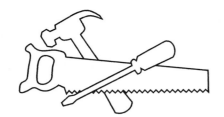

A
METASTRATEGIC
APPROACH
TO LEARNING
TO LEARN

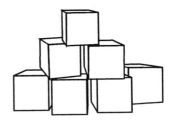

Using Metastrategic Knowledge

In the Cognitive Enrichment Advantage (CEA) metastrategic approach, students develop the knowledge needed to construct their own personally relevant learning strategies for use in any learning experience. Students use their metastrategic knowledge—cognitive, affective, and motivational information—to build learning strategies. The information becomes *meta* when learners use it to think about their thinking related to knowledge they use to build strategies. To help them develop these personal learning strategies, members of the laboratory for learning use Building Blocks of Thinking and Tools of Learning, which emphasize important aspects of cognition, affect, and motivation.

The twelve Building Blocks of Thinking, with their focus on cognitive processes, foster effective thinking. Building Blocks of Thinking provide insight into three important areas of effective cognitive functioning: approaching the learning experience, making meaning of the learning experience, and confirming the learning experience (see Figure 3.1). The eight Tools of Learning focus on learners' feelings about and commitment and attitude toward learning. These affective-motivational approaches foster independent and interdependent learning when used effectively.

To set the stage for use of the Building Blocks and Tools by the classroom community, the CEA comprehensive teaching method helps teacher-mediators create a highly nurturing environment where students can more easily gain insight into planning and monitoring their own learning strategies. This supportive environ-

---

FIGURE 3.1

Categories of CEA Metastrategic Knowledge

Building Blocks of Thinking (cognitive processes that foster effective thinking)

❑ Approaching the learning experience (exploring, planning, expressing thoughts and actions)

❑ Making meaning of the learning experience (retrieving, comparing, synthesizing, relating, integrating, and comparing ideas)

❑ Confirming the learning experience (clarifying, validating, correcting, and defining needs)

Tools of Learning (affective-motivational approaches that foster independent and interdependent learning)

❑ Understanding feelings within the learning experience (optimizing the positive effect of emotions that accompany thoughts and actions and impact values)

❑ Motivating behavior within the learning experience (choosing, initiating, and persisting in specific actions)

ment is important because learners gain the most insight when they are in the zone of proximal development and aware of the need for assistance.

The Outcome of a Metastrategic Approach

CEA teacher-mediators encourage students to develop flexibility in thinking that can help them see beyond a problem to a solution and accept responsibility for the choices they make. Through mediated learning experiences, students engage with teacher-mediators in questioning the process of learning, challenging and justifying choices, searching for patterns, and seeking relationships.

CEA students learn how to think about their strategic thinking. They learn how to experience and define problems, focus on relevant information, make comparisons, approach tasks systematically, integrate thoughts, get the main idea, and manage their working memories. They develop an appreciation for the need to have a precise understanding of what they know and to share that knowledge accurately. CEA students learn to connect the present learning experience to learning experiences in the past and future. They understand how time and space concepts affect almost all learning.

CEA students also develop metastrategic knowledge to help them understand how feelings impact learning. Emotions are connected to thoughts and actions, to cognition and motivation. The Tools focus on understanding feelings that impact learning and helping students focus on positive aspects of these emotions. They learn they can draw on feelings that energize learning and provide the learning experience with meaning. Through the CEA teaching method, students learn how to overcome the negative aspects of challenge and anticipate and find pleasure in challenge, seeing it as positive and exciting. They become aware of how they have changed and of their beliefs about their abilities, which lead to beliefs about success or failure. This awareness helps them understand and gain control over these beliefs so they can say, "I am a person who can do this task."

CEA students also focus on motivation, that important ability to choose, initiate, and persist in actions. By understanding self-regulation, goal orientation, self-development, and sharing behavior, they learn to construct strategies that lead to more effective independent and interdependent learning.

An Overview of Building Blocks and Tools

The Building Blocks of Thinking and Tools of Learning are based on metastrategic knowledge and derived from theory, research, and classroom application. All of the Building Blocks and Tools are related to the cognitive deficiencies described by Feuerstein (Feuerstein et al. 1980) in his theory of mediated learning experience. Some of the cognitive processes that compose the Building Blocks have been the subject of much research such as Selective Attention, Working Memory, and the use of simultaneous and sequential coding of the Building Block of Thought Integration. Other concepts in this section on Building Blocks and Tools are theoretical in nature. Not every idea related to the contribution of a Building Block or Tool to learning has, to date, been thoroughly investigated with highly controlled studies. Because of the apparent interwoven effects of these cognitive processes and affective-motivational approaches, it is very difficult to conduct research that demonstrates their interdependence and importance in learning. Until resources and methodologies are available to do so, formal theory and practitioners' personal theories guide the selection and revision of CEA Building Blocks and Tools at least as much as research studies do.

Figure 3.2 lists CEA's twelve Building Blocks of Thinking that represent most of the cognitive functions or processes Feuerstein defines (Feuerstein et al. 1980). Figure 3.3 lists CEA's Tools of Learning that represent most of the characteristics of mediated learning experience Feuerstein describes. The Tools focus more directly on understanding feelings and motivating behavior within a learning experience.

Using Labels for Building Blocks and Tools

The Building Blocks of Thinking and Tools of Learning are grouped somewhat arbitrarily into five categories: three categories address cognitive needs, one category focuses on affect, and another addresses motivational needs. The purpose of this organization—three cognitive categories for the Building Blocks and two affect and motivation categories for the Tools—is to facilitate student memory and learning. In reality, many Building Blocks and Tools contain aspects that fit all three areas of cognition, affect, and motivation. These five categories emphasize the importance of considering all three areas as one seeks to become a more effective independent and interdependent learner.

When teaching the Building Blocks of Thinking and the Tools of Learning, it is imperative to use the labels for each concept and its category. It is only through the use of labels that students (and teachers) are able to build a shared vocabulary they can use to create personal learning strategies. No matter how clearly students understand the meaning of each Building Block and Tool, this knowledge is of little use in building metastrategic knowledge unless students have a name for each concept and understand how it fits into its given category. Therefore, even with younger and lower functioning learners, it is critically important to use the labels for each Building Block and Tool and the categories.

Although teachers sometimes feel challenged by the labels, students almost never avoid their use. In fact, students are usually eager to share this new vocabulary with family members and others whom they wish to impress. Certain practices help students and teachers learn the labels more readily. For example, teachers should display illustrations in this chapter and icons (see Appendix) in the class-

FIGURE 3.2

CEA Building Blocks of Thinking

Building Blocks for *Approaching the Learning Experience*

Exploration	to search systematically for information needed in the learning experience
Planning	to prepare and use an organized approach in the learning experience
Expression	to communicate thoughts and actions carefully in the learning experience

Building Blocks for *Making Meaning of the Learning Experience*

Working Memory	to use memory processes effectively
Making Comparisons	to discover similarities and differences automatically among some parts of the learning experience
Getting the Main Idea	to identify the basic thought that holds related ideas together
Thought Integration	to combine pieces of information into complete thoughts and hold onto them while needed
Connecting Events	to find relationships among past, present, and future learning experiences automatically

Building Blocks for *Confirming the Learning Experience*

Precision and Accuracy	to know there is a need to understand words and concepts and use them correctly and to seek information automatically when the need arises
Space and Time Concepts	to understand and use information about space and time that is important in almost all learning
Selective Attention	to choose between relevant and irrelevant information and to focus on the information needed in the learning experience
Problem Identification	to experience a sense of imbalance automatically and define its cause when something interferes with successful learning

room. They provide a permanent reference when a class member needs help identifying or remembering a label. They also encourage students to think more broadly about the need for more than one Building Block or Tool in a given learning experience. With these visual reminders, students often find it easier to find what can help them in a given situation as well as see the many ways that Building Blocks and Tools work together.

To assist teacher-mediators in understanding the similarities and differences between Building Blocks of Thinking and Tools of Learning, the next two sections focus on the distinguishing features of Building Blocks of Thinking and Tools of Learning and on how they relate to one another.

FIGURE 3.3

CEA Tools of Learning

Tools for *Understanding Feelings within the Learning Experience*

Inner Meaning — to seek deep, personal value in learning experiences that energizes thinking and behavior and leads to greater commitment and success

Feeling of Challenge — to energize learning in new and complex experiences by focusing on the learning process rather than fear and anxiety about a possible unsuccessful product

Awareness of Self-Change — to recognize and understand feelings related to personal growth and to learn to expect and welcome change and development

Feeling of Competence — to energize feelings, thoughts, and behaviors by developing beliefs about being capable of learning and doing something effectively

Tools for *Motivating Behavior within the Learning Experience*

Self-Regulation — to reflect on thoughts and actions as they occur to energize, sustain, and direct behavior toward successful learning and doing

Goal Orientation — to take purposeful action in consistently setting, seeking, and reaching personal objectives

Self-Development — to appreciate special qualities in everyone and to enhance personal potential

Sharing Behavior — to energize life and learning for everyone by sharing thoughts and actions through effective interdependent learning skills

The Relationship of Building Blocks to Affective-Motivational Approaches

The Building Blocks of Thinking comprise twelve cognitive processes that foster effective thinking. They were derived from the description by Feuerstein of twenty-eight cognitive deficiencies that interfere with effective learning for people of all ages and at all levels of intellectual functioning (Feuerstein et al. 1980). The twelve Building Blocks have descriptive names suitable for use with learners of all ages and levels of functioning. Students also learn to label the problems that result from ineffective use of the Building Blocks. Learners find it very helpful to explore various degrees of effectiveness in the use of each Building Block of Thinking on a continuum from highly effective to highly ineffective cognitive processing. Students like to explore the various behaviors one might display at each level along the continuum. For example, a student approaching the task of baking a cake might use impulsive Exploration and not search carefully for items needed at the grocery

store, forgetting some important ingredients and giving up when she can't find others. Or she could check every shelf and item systematically until she finds all she needs.

All learners vary from one task to another in the degree of effectiveness with which they use strategies based on a given Building Block of Thinking. According to Feuerstein, the content of the domain, or subject matter, the modality in which the task is presented, the level of abstractness, and other factors affect this fluctuation (Feuerstein et al. 1980).

Research demonstrates the close association of affect and motivation with learning and academic performance (Schunk and Zimmerman 1994); for example, some students display a stronger aptitude for language skills than for mathematics. If these students have experienced failure with mathematics in the past, their negative beliefs about their ability (self-efficacy) to learn math may lead to less cognitive engagement with the task; for example, they are more passive in approaching the task and use fewer Building Blocks and Tools to help them succeed. The value they place on learning mathematics also affects these students' engagement with the task and consequent use of learning strategies. In some research, cognitive strategy use and self-regulation predicted performance directly. In other studies, values appeared to influence strategy use more directly. What is most important to remember about the variation in effective use of strategies developed from Building Blocks of Thinking is students can change a failure cycle themselves.

To reverse a cycle of failure, students must develop metastrategic knowledge they can use to construct learning strategies that improve their cognitive processing and affective-motivational approach to the learning experience. Students need to learn labels and actively seek to understand Building Blocks and Tools and how learners use them to build strategies. They must be willing to think of strategies and try them out. When students know the Building Blocks and Tools, they can determine how one or more can help them, then plan a strategy using the appropriate Building Block or Tool for the particular situation. Most students need support to be successful initially. In the nurturing environment the CEA teaching method helps teacher-mediators create, underachieving students can give up the belief that they are unlucky when they fail and lucky when they succeed.

The Relationship of Tools of Learning to Cognitive Processes

The eight Tools of Learning focus on affective-motivational approaches that foster independent and interdependent learning. Derived from Feuerstein's parameters of mediated learning, the Tools provide an important, holistic balance to the Building Blocks of Thinking; they are the glue that holds the Building Blocks together (Feuerstein et al. 1980).

Eggan and Kauchak define motivation as "a force that energizes, sustains, and directs behavior toward a goal" (1997, 341). They state that figuring out how to deal with motivation problems is one of the biggest concerns of teachers. All the Tools of Learning can help teachers address this concern by giving students tools they can use to overcome motivation problems for themselves.

To overcome these problems, students need more than the four Tools that focus on motivating behaviors within the learning experience; they also need the four Tools for understanding feelings. Emotions energize the factors of motivation (choosing, initiating, and persisting in specific actions), and both emotion and motivation interact very closely with cognition. People think differently when they are upset, and, certainly, the thoughts they have about a situation affect the feelings they have about the situation. For example, a student who fails a test may think he does not have the ability to master the subject of the test. His thoughts include the reaction of family members and friends as they learn about his failure. It is very important for teachers to understand how closely cognition, affect, and motivation work together.

The Role of Tools of Learning in Overcoming Affective-Motivational Problems

The relationship among affect, motivation, and cognition indicates that successful learning involves much more than learners finding a cognitive strategy to help them memorize facts. Teacher-mediators who want to help students understand and overcome learning problems must think about many factors that may influence performance. The Tools of Learning can play a crucial role. For example, Schunk and Zimmerman describe the importance of student valuing or, in CEA terms, finding an inner meaning for a learning experience (1994). Students who do not use the Tool of Inner Meaning are much less likely to be engaged in the task and even less likely to use or develop learning strategies related to the task. In addition, teacher-mediators must be sensitive to the relationship between cultural values and the Tools of Learning.

Cultural Values and Tools of Learning

Feuerstein states that parameters of mediated learning are mediated to learners based on the cultural values of their parents and other caregivers (Feuerstein et al. 1980). The caregivers share only those parameters the culture values. Klein (1995) describes her study of the differences in parent mediation with young children in different cultural settings. For example, some cultures value the development of individuation (what CEA calls Self-Development) more than other cultures do. Many Eastern cultures value more the ability of a person to fit within a family or

part of society. Therefore, teacher-mediators must be sensitive to family values concerning the Tools of Learning and explore with students differing views.

Fostering Independent and Interdependent Learning

The Tools of Learning are designed to help students become highly effective independent and interdependent learners. Independent learning involves the ability and skill to generate information actively and regulate one's own thoughts and actions in ways that allow one to participate effectively in learning experiences. Interdependent learning involves the ability and skill to learn collaboratively with others, display social skills that allow one to contribute effectively within a learning community, and facilitate the collaborative and independent learning of others. Highly effective teacher-mediators who facilitate the social construction of knowledge are also effective interdependent learners. Covey (1989) makes the important point that successful independent functioning and character building precedes effective interdependence. Indeed, one can only contribute to the learning community what one possesses. This does not mean, however, that students are unable to engage successfully in collaborative and cooperative learning activities until they become highly effective independent learners. CEA teacher-mediators report that carefully planned interdependent activities help students gain independent learning skills—interdependent and independent activities are mutually beneficial. This is especially true when teacher-mediators and some members of each small group demonstrate effective independent learning.

For teacher-mediators to help students develop into good independent and interdependent learners, they must provide plenty of opportunities for students to be independent and interdependent. Dependent and codependent behaviors result when teacher-mediators take too much control of learning activities, the behavior of class members, and the knowledge constructed within the activities; provide the most important or only feedback on projects completed by class members; or spend the majority of class time attempting to transmit knowledge to students instead of facilitating mediated learning experiences. When all class members learn to ask questions more than they provide answers, inquire into others' ideas more than they advocate their own, and respect learning opportunities for all learners rather than taking over for others when learning problems occur, then independent and interdependent learning is nurtured and not hindered.

Recognizing Ineffective Use of Building Blocks and Tools

It is critically important that teacher-mediators recognize ineffective use of the Building Blocks and Tools. CEA is a highly effective approach to use with underachieving students, but some students need assistance recognizing those areas in which they most need to develop strategies that can overcome specific cognitive processing or affective-motivational problems. When teacher-mediators can recognize characteristics of ineffective use, they can focus student attention on that concept and assist the student in developing a strategy for the given situation.

Effective use leads to effective independent and interdependent learning. Ineffective use leads to bad habits for learning that interfere with success and capacity building. Students should also learn to recognize differences in effective and ineffective use of Building Blocks of Thinking and Tools of Learning. They identify each by learning about them through minilessons their teachers use and watching for them in their own learning and that of other people. Even very young students notice others' use of Building Blocks and Tools at ineffective and effective levels.

Only occasionally do students use a Building Block perfectly or at a totally ineffective level. The use of Building Blocks and Tools occurs on a continuum from highly effective to highly ineffective. The goal is for learners to move toward more effective use more often and to be aware of the availability of metastrategic knowledge they possess about the Building Blocks and Tools, which they can use to overcome challenges in the process of learning. They have learned, tried out, and stored this information, which is available as they need it to solve problems.

The degree of effectiveness with which a learner uses each Building Block or Tool changes based on many factors related to the learning experience. A learner may display a highly effective level of a Building Block or Tool on one occasion and a much lower level on another, in part due to the content of the task. For example, a student may use Exploration systematically during a math lesson and Exploration impulsively during a reading lesson on the same day. The goal of the teacher-mediator is to help students become aware of their ability to use Building Blocks or Tools effectively in some situations and to transfer that ability to other situations where they use the Building Block or Tool less effectively.

When teacher-mediators first attempt to diagnose ineffective use of a given Building Block or Tool, they sometimes become frustrated if they cannot find the one right answer. It is not important that teachers identify the only Building Block or Tool a student needs most. Instead, it is important to identify a few possibilities and allow the student to select the one that seems most relevant. In time, students become very clear in their choices. Teacher-mediators still need to observe for ineffective use so they can select relevant Building Blocks or Tools or minilessons for spontaneous mediation.

Building Blocks of Thinking

The following section assists teacher-mediators in facilitating students' development of metastrategic knowledge by highlighting various levels of effectiveness in the use of each Building Block. The Building Blocks are divided into three categories: approaching the learning experience, making meaning of the learning experience, and confirming the learning experience. The discussion of each Building Block provides information on the role the Building Block plays in learning, a description of its effective use, examples of ineffective use, and tips on how to mediate each Building Block. Two tips apply to every Building Block:

- ❏ Use minilessons to help students develop metastrategic knowledge about the specific Building Block. (Found in the *Cognitive Enrichment Advantage Minilessons,* the minilessons offer teachers guidelines for integrating the Building Blocks and Tools into the school curriculum.)

- ❏ Use bridging to help students develop decontextualized principles and examples of strategies related to the principles they can use in a variety of situations where they need this specific Building Block.

An explanation of the use of minilessons and bridging appears in chapter 4.

Approaching the Learning Experience

The three Building Blocks for approaching the learning experience are Exploration, Planning, and Expression.

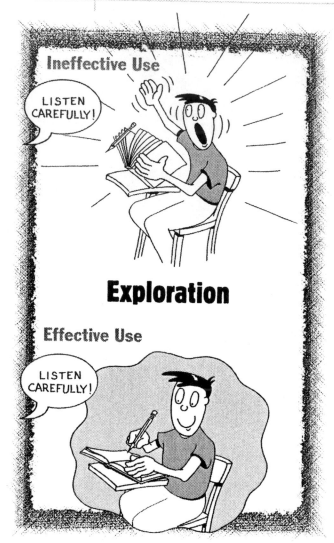

EXPLORATION

Key Concepts

To search systematically for information needed in the learning experience

Effective use: systematic Exploration, careful search

Ineffective use: impulsive Exploration, careless search, lack of awareness of need to gather information

Effective Use of Exploration

❏ Search carefully, not impulsively.

❏ Gather necessary information, not all the information available.

❏ Gather all necessary information, not just some information.

When approaching any challenging learning experience, learners need to gather carefully all the information or materials they need for success. School activities are often overly organized, so many students have no need to develop strategies for Exploration. For example, a common task is a grammar activity that requires students to find and correct specific errors. Every sentence in the activity has only one type of error, such as subject-verb agreement; students have no reason to search systematically for all kinds of errors. Because the real world does not provide this kind of assistance, learners must know how to search in an orderly manner for information and materials they need. Exploration helps learning become effective because learners cannot complete most tasks without gathering all the needed information. When they use Exploration effectively, students avoid wasting time for they do not discover midway through a task that they have not gathered all the necessary information.

Sometimes learners need to gather information from one or more sources that may or may not be readily available. Effective learning depends on learners' ability to develop a strategy that ensures systematic Exploration based on the needs of a specific situation. Many strategies for using Exploration systematically are possible as long as the strategies ensure that learners have all needed information as they plan the approach to the learning experience and express the results of learning.

Recognizing Ineffective Use of Exploration

The degree of effectiveness with which learners use Exploration ranges from highly systematic to highly impulsive. Impulsive Exploration of a learning experience is easy to observe because it greatly affects students' ability to complete the learning experience successfully, and students usually make a number of mistakes. It involves acting without reflection, often in a hurried manner. Some students may be unaware of the need to gather information even when information or materials are carefully organized and presented. These students may ignore the materials provided, jump into the learning experience, and start a task without even thinking about checking that they have what they need to complete the task. While some students are unaware of the need to develop a strategy for systematic Exploration, others simply may not know how to develop such a strategy. They may explore to a certain extent but move into the task after a careless search in which they gather only part of what they need.

Examples of Ineffective Exploration

- ❏ A student blurts out an answer to a question before the speaker completes the question.

- ❏ A student who has lost her gloves looks for them by rushing from one place to another in a disorganized manner.

- ❏ A student begins working without reading the directions.

- ❏ A team finishes its project much more quickly than other teams, and someone points out that they omitted a major part of the task.

- ❏ Team members are not working well together and appear confused about what they want to do.

Tips for Mediating Exploration

- ■ Encourage students to listen to others carefully.

- ■ Establish an expectation in the classroom that all learners take time to reflect before responding or seeking additional information.

- ■ Ask questions that focus on how students or teams used Exploration to help them be successful in a learning experience.

- ■ Monitor activities to ensure they challenge students appropriately and consistently with the need to explore systematically gathering information or materials. To challenge students, for example, omit instructions from handouts so students learn to infer what to do, or make teams responsible for gathering all the supplies they need before beginning to work on a project and for justifying the need for any additional supplies.

PLANNING

Key Concepts

To prepare and use an organized approach in the learning experience

Effective use: organized Planning, systematic Planning, deliberate approach

Ineffective use: inadequate Planning, lack of Planning behavior, lack of awareness of the need for Planning

Effective Use of Planning

❑ Think about the goal.

❑ Decide on the steps of the plan for reaching the goal and their order.

❑ Make changes to the plan when needed.

Planning is an important part of approaching a learning experience. Learners develop a plan after gathering all needed information or supplies with a strategy for Exploration. They use the information they have about the learning experience to determine appropriate actions or desired outcomes. Then they sequence events or procedures in an order effective for the given situation. Plans vary in the degree of detail based on the complexity of the learning situation and the preferences and needs of the individual or team using the plan. Effective learners implement plans in a flexible manner, reflecting on the usefulness of the plan during its use (through Self-Regulation) and making changes as necessary. Planning helps control impulsive behavior.

Recognizing Ineffective Use of Planning

Because teachers cannot observe students' thinking, they must infer inadequate Planning behavior or lack of Planning from learners' actions (written plans are an exception). Impulsive learners seldom engage in Planning behavior. Often these learners are unsuccessful in the learning experience because, unaware of the need for organized Planning, they omit steps that would have helped them achieve a successful outcome.

Some learners have difficulty understanding the importance of sequencing the steps of a plan. These students may develop inadequate plans with only one or two

steps that may not lead clearly to the desired outcome. Some of their plans may have more steps but no logical order to the steps.

Examples of Ineffective Planning

- ❏ A student cannot adequately predict the outcome of her behavior in a given situation.

- ❏ A student has difficulty stating a goal for a project.

- ❏ Team members know what they want to accomplish but cannot explain what they need to do to reach their goal.

- ❏ Team members are frustrated because they realize no one has been keeping notes about the ideas they are generating.

Tips for Mediating Planning

- ■ Encourage students to determine desired outcomes and then steps for reaching the outcome when engaged in any challenging activity.

- ■ Establish expectations in the classroom for students to share plans for working and to justify the steps in their plans with regard to appropriate sequence and effectiveness in reaching the desired outcome.

- ■ Ask questions that help students compare plans and justify differences and similarities based on the situation.

- ■ Monitor team and individual work to ensure that students modify plans as needed.

EXPRESSION

Key Concepts

To communicate thoughts and actions carefully in the learning experience

Effective use: controlled Expression, careful Expression of thoughts and actions, thoughtful communication

Ineffective use: impulsive Expression, careless Expression, lack of awareness of the need for controlled Expression

Effective Use of Expression

❏ Communicate clearly and with control.

❏ Express everything needed to share thoughts and actions.

❏ Express thoughts and actions in the order intended.

Systematic Exploration and organized Planning are not enough to ensure a successful learning experience unless students can express what they learned in a controlled manner. Learners need to plan and monitor clear communication, whether through oral, written, or some other form of Expression, to ensure that it represents what the learner wishes to express accurately and effectively. Learners and recipients of their communication benefit from controlled Expression: clear communication facilitates further interaction based on the learners' and recipients' reflection and understanding of the communication. Controlled Expression facilitates collaborative learning through careful communication that allows everyone time to reflect on what learners share. Controlled Expression also helps learners evaluate skills in the area of communication—making an oral or written presentation, drawing, acting, dancing, and so on.

Recognizing Ineffective Use of Expression

The impulsive Expression of thoughts and actions related to a learning experience is sometimes confused with other learning problems. When teachers suspect it, they need to find out whether the learner's problem is one of not sharing his thoughts and actions effectively, or a problem with some other aspect of the learn-

ing experience has led to an inadequate response. In some situations, a learner displays careless Expression in one modality but not another or is unaware of the need for controlled Expression. Sometimes egocentric communication, especially in young students, appears to be impulsive Expression when it actually is a problem with Precision and Accuracy.

As with impulsive Exploration, impulsive Expression occurs when learners do not take time to reflect before responding. This form of impulsiveness is particularly frustrating for learners when they know what they want to communicate but realize they have not adequately controlled the way in which they communicate, and others misunderstand them.

If learners correct the expressed response spontaneously without assistance, the problem is most likely controlled Expression. In such circumstances, learners may need minimal assistance to develop strategies that lead to systematic Exploration.

Examples of Ineffective Expression

- ❑ A student gets mixed up while relating something that happened to her that she clearly understands.

- ❑ A student makes many careless errors.

- ❑ A student responds correctly when asked to share a response orally but incorrectly when asked to share a response in writing.

- ❑ A team works very hard on an effective plan for a project and then presents incomplete results.

Tips for Mediating Expression

- ■ Encourage students to question the process they and others use to determine how they express a response to a learning experience.

- ■ Establish expectations in the classroom for high standards regarding the sharing of results of a learning experience. Focus attention on the process used to achieve effective Expression.

- ■ Allow a clear amount of wait-time for class members to think carefully before responding to teacher or classmates' questions.

- ■ Observe students and teams as they prepare responses and help them think about using controlled Expression.

Making Meaning of the Learning Experience

The five Building Blocks for making meaning of the learning experience are Working Memory, Making Comparisons, Getting the Main Idea, Thought Integration, and Connecting Events.

WORKING MEMORY

Key Concepts

To use memory processes effectively

Effective use: skillful use of Working Memory, well-developed use of Working Memory

Ineffective use: impaired working memory, limited management of working memory

Effective Use of Working Memory

- ❑ Clear thoughts and feelings from the working memory that distract from the learning experience.

- ❑ Focus energy on recalling information stored in the brain, combining new and old ideas, and storing newly integrated thoughts in the brain.

- ❑ Use all the space available in the working memory.

Memory is a powerful and important part of thinking and learning. It involves the processes in the brain that allow storage and retrieval of information and its integration with new ideas.

The Building Block of Working Memory focuses on managing memory processes skillfully. It involves making meaning of the learning experience by clearing distractions from the mind, focusing energy on thinking, and remembering and retrieving old information and integrating and storing old and new information in the brain. Although theories abound about the actual processes occurring in the memory, most theorists agree that a good analogy for memory, at least simplistically, is a computer's random access memory (RAM), which stores and retrieves information and allows users to make changes in that information.

The Building Block of Working Memory aids learners in developing strategies that can help their working memory function more effectively. Many learners are pleasantly surprised to learn they can do a great deal to improve the functioning of their working memory once they understand the affective-motivational factors that affect its functioning and some of its processes, including its need for energy and its need for space.

When learners become mindful of the sensation that occurs when they increase energy to the working memory, they can take control and monitor memory tasks in ways that increase effectiveness. They can use Inner Meaning and Feeling of Competence to increase their interest in the learning experience and belief in their ability to become an effective learner. When students are aware that working memory space can become overloaded, especially with feelings of worry and anxiety, they can use Feeling of Competence and Feeling of Challenge to gain control over anxiety. Through the use of Selective Attention, they can decide what information is relevant and focus on it and remove their attention from irrelevant information.

Automaticity affects the working memory. Poor readers, for example, who must use working memory space to decode words have less space as well as energy for comprehension. In contrast, good readers have more working memory space available for understanding and integrating a text's ideas.

Recognizing Ineffective Use of Working Memory

The ineffective use of Working Memory can result in students engaging in more concrete and less abstract thinking, which is also the case when working memory is actually impaired. Unless teacher-mediators and students make an effort to use strategies to improve working memory function, students may be thought to have a learning disability, even brain damage. When a student has a lot on his or her mind, such as problems causing anxiety, little space is left for learning activities, and the usual result is ineffective learning. Ample space must be available for thinking if students are to become effective independent learners.

If a student's use of memory in areas of interest to him or her, such as an impressive ability to remember sports statistics, reveals an adequate or even excellent memory in those select areas, then a teacher-mediator can have more confidence in the student's abilities and expect faster change as she works with the student to develop strategies to improve use of Working Memory in areas that hold less personal value for the student.

In every case, teacher-mediators should assume students can improve their use of Working Memory and strive to facilitate students' development of strategies, rather than lower expectations for learning. As long as teacher-mediators provide a nurturing environment, the positive stress that results from high expectations may result in significant improvement in use of Working Memory (see also Figure 3.4).

FIGURE 3.4

Tips for Rote Memorization

Note: While effectiveness in engaging in rote memory tasks can be improved through a mediated learning focus on strategies to increase the effectiveness of Working Memory use, other kinds of mediated learning activities such as seeking relationships during the memorization process can actually interfere. For example, a common strategy for helping students memorize math facts is to say, "If you know 5 x 4, then you can figure out 5 x 5." Attempting to establish relationships actually interferes with memorizing. Rote memory tasks, such as learning math facts or memorizing vocabulary terms, are best accomplished with two students working together, coaching each other and providing the correct response as soon after an incorrect response as possible. Repetition of the responses should continue until students are able to share correct responses orally in a very few seconds (for math facts, in less than two seconds) or write correct responses in no more than twice the amount of time expected for the oral response. Interactions in which students are expected to connect events or integrate thoughts, for example to better comprehend the concepts of multiplication, are an important part of learning but need to take place separately from rote memorization.

Examples of Ineffective Working Memory

- ❏ A student is distracted and not paying close attention when information is shared about a major school event.

- ❏ A student who claims to be unable to memorize math facts can easily share the phone numbers of her many friends.

- ❏ A student is having a difficult time dealing with a family crisis and fails a test that included many items requiring recall of learned information.

- ❏ A student who knew math facts last week can't remember them this week.

- ❏ A student is asked to summarize what the class did in reading class the day before. The student listens to the question, then looks confused and does not respond.

- ❏ A student whose mother is critically ill cannot complete assignments on time and makes mistakes she seldom did before her mother's illness.

Tips for Mediating Working Memory

■ Tell students who are distracted by thoughts unrelated to the present learning experience to focus briefly but intently on those irrelevant thoughts, then "wipe them away" with the downward motion of the hand.

■ Ask questions to determine whether a student with memory problems has an effective use of memory in other areas. Help the student find Inner Meaning that can improve use of Working Memory in an area in which the student experiences difficulty.

■ Reflect with students on the sensations they should experience when really striving to put energy into storing information in their brain or retrieving information from long-term memory.

MAKING COMPARISONS

Key Concepts

To discover similarities and differences automatically among some parts of the learning experience

Effective use: Making Comparisons automatically, awareness of need for Making Comparisons

Ineffective use: lack of awareness of need for Making Comparisons, Making Comparisons inadequately

Effective Use of Making Comparisons

❑ Know a need exists for Making Comparisons.

❑ Make comparisons automatically without having to think hard to do so.

❑ Think about how two or more objects are the same as or different from each other or some standard and make meaning in the learning situation.

❑ Compare thoughts and actions with expectations.

Virtually no thinking occurs without Making Comparisons. This Building Block underlies and assists all others. Making Comparisons is one of the most fundamental Building Blocks of higher level thinking. It is necessary for determining relationships among objects, ideas, and events. People who compare automatically are much more successful in a learning situation than those who do not.

From a very early age, learners have the ability to compare. Doing it automatically is quite another matter. Learners who are proficient in Making Comparisons use this Building Block spontaneously. This Building Block helps students understand that they need to use it spontaneously in all learning experiences.

It is important to recognize that comparisons always involve some kind of standard of comparison. For example, if someone describes a pencil as big, that person is most likely comparing it with the common size of pencils. If someone says a party was a really good one, she has compared the party with other parties and has decided this party is different or better than the average party.

Recognizing Ineffective Use of Making Comparisons

The most common manifestation of ineffective use of Making Comparisons occurs when students do not notice their careless errors. In such cases, the students have not compared their responses with what they expected to communicate. Unable to compare their results with the teacher's expectations or task objectives, students with this ineffective level of functioning also may not recognize they are completing a task correctly unless the teacher-mediator tell them so. They are unaware that they have standards available in their memory they can use to look for similarities and differences automatically.

Examples of Ineffective Making Comparisons

❏ Asked to compare two rooms (a classroom and a room at home), students notice only color and room size differences. They notice both rooms have chairs but they don't recognize that the chairs and their use are different, or they recognize both rooms have lights, but they don't point out that the classroom has overhead fluorescent lights and the room in the home has floor lamps.

❏ A student asks constantly, "Is this right, teacher?" when a model he could compare with is available.

❏ Team members are unaware they have made another student angry because they have not compared her behavioral cues with signs of anger.

❏ Students do not notice the room has been rearranged.

Tips for Mediating Making Comparisons

■ Encourage students to evaluate their own performance continually and provide them with insight into their natural need to compare their work with some standard they have established in memory.

■ Establish expectations for students to catch careless errors.

■ Ask questions and encourage students to ask each other about the standards they use to make comparisons.

■ Monitor teamwork to determine if members are Making Comparisons to determine how well they work as a team. They should make comparisons with standards provided through class discussion about what is good teamwork.

GETTING THE MAIN IDEA

Key Concepts
To identify the basic thought that holds related ideas together

Effective use: clearly Getting the Main Idea, finding the basic concept

Ineffective use: inadequate use of Getting the Main Idea, impaired ability to get the main idea

Effective Use of Getting the Main Idea

❑ Look for relationships among objects, events, and actions.

❑ Look for the basic thought that holds related ideas together.

❑ Look for the main idea automatically.

An important aspect of forming relationships is the ability to determine the fundamental element that connects ideas. Seeking relationships among ideas is essential to all but the simplest forms of learning. Use of the Building Block of Getting the Main Idea enhances the determination of appropriate relationships among concepts, relationships based on relevant associations that are logical or natural. Students also learn that they can form relationships among ideas in a learning experience that will not help them make meaning of a learning experience.

When students read a story, try to "get" a joke, or seek understanding of a class activity, their learning is greatly affected by their ability to get the main idea. When they see value in finding the elemental thought that two or more ideas have in common, they can understand and make meaning of the learning experience more fully. For example, students reading a story are able to see how the events flow one into the other; however, the story takes on a much deeper meaning when they also see that, together, the events make a statement about how to treat others as they would like to be treated. As a result, they think about the story differently and can compare this story with others in a more appropriate manner.

Teachers frequently need to challenge students to find main ideas. Students must learn how to reflect on the appropriateness of the suggested main idea within the learning experience. When they use Getting the Main Idea inadequately, students need more time and assistance to understand why the response is inadequate and how to look across relationships to find the main idea.

Students need to use several other Building Blocks of Thinking for success in Getting the Main Idea: they must be able to combine information into an organized unit, using the Building Block of Thought Integration. They must also be aware of the need for Making Comparisons, and they must use Working Memory.

Recognizing Ineffective Use of Getting the Main Idea

If learners seem confused about what to do and stop working or ask questions that demonstrate little meaningful understanding; if they do not see the relationship between two pieces of information and, as a result, change the purpose of the task or omit important parts; if they have no apparent need to pull ideas together to get a clear picture of the task and show little interest in persisting with the task; they are displaying ineffective use of Getting the Main Idea.

Examples of Ineffective Getting the Main Idea

- ❏ A student cannot get to the point of the story she is sharing with the class.

- ❏ A student almost never understands or "gets" jokes.

- ❏ After reading a story successfully, the student has difficulty suggesting an appropriate title for the work.

- ❏ A student acts as though she has never studied the mathematics concepts that are a part of the lesson when, in reality, the lesson introduces only one new aspect of regrouping in subtraction.

- ❏ When a team member who has just returned to the group shares new information, the team members do not appreciate the contribution because they do not see how the information fits the main idea of the project.

Tips for Mediating Getting the Main Idea

Note: Some learners may need to improve skills in Making Comparisons before focusing on Getting the Main Idea.

- **Encourage students to seek relationships among ideas automatically.**

- **Establish an expectation in the classroom that sharing the relationship among ideas is a highly valued contribution to everyone's learning.**

- **Ask questions that help learners develop a need to discover relationships among pieces of information.**

- **Monitor teamwork to ensure that all members of a group can share the fundamental idea behind their project.**

THOUGHT INTEGRATION

Key Concepts

To combine pieces of information into complete thoughts and hold onto them while needed

> **Effective use:** spontaneous use of Thought Integration, effective use of simultaneous and sequential processing

> **Ineffective use:** inadequate use of Thought Integration, inadequate use of simultaneous and sequential processing, lack of awareness of need for Thought Integration

Effective Use of Thought Integration

- ❏ Combine all bits of information needed to form a whole idea.

- ❏ Hold onto all the bits of information needed while working.

- ❏ Be aware of the need to combine bits of information.

An important and basic part of processing necessary information to make meaning within a learning experience, Thought Integration

Ineffective Use

a Cat s it on the cHAir.

Thought Integration

Effective Use

A cat sits on the chair.

focuses on pulling together small pieces of necessary information. Thought Integration involves two different forms of processing information, or coding (Das, Naglieri, and Kirby 1994): simultaneous coding requires the synthesis of pieces of information into a combined whole, and sequential coding requires the consideration of data in a series, one bit of information after the other.

Thinking almost always involves a focus on more than one piece of information at a time. During a learning experience, information comes to the learner from several sources, either simultaneously or sequentially. For example, a busy person is planning a dinner party. A successful dinner requires a plan, and an effective plan requires the person's awareness of the need to consider multiple sources of information automatically: 1. who is coming, 2. what they are willing to eat, 3. what he wants to cook, and 4. additional factors such as a soup bowl broken last week means not enough bowls to have soup on the menu. The host needs to process some of this information simultaneously (what the guests are willing to eat, what the host wants to cook), while other pieces of information he must code sequentially (each guest). If the host combines information into complete thoughts within the event, his planning will be more successful.

The ability to use Thought Integration to combine pieces of information into a complete thought occurs with the use of Working Memory and Making Comparisons.

Recognizing Ineffective Use of Thought Integration

Learners use Thought Integration ineffectively more frequently than any other Building Block. Because it causes mistakes or the inability to complete a task, teachers may confuse ineffective use of this Building Block with impulsiveness. For example, a student is asked to complete a math computation such as 284-159 and gets an answer of 135. The teacher-mediator needs to determine whether the problem is due to the student not using Thought Integration to combine information about subtracting the larger number 9 from the smaller number 4. If students do not use simultaneous or sequential processing appropriately by considering every source of information necessary within the event, then ineffective use of Thought Integration has most likely occurred. For most learners, however, ineffective use is due to lack of awareness of the need to use Thought Integration spontaneously all the time rather than an inability to engage in the process.

Learners who have difficulty processing information simultaneously or sequentially also have difficulty forming relationships among pieces of information and Getting the Main Idea. These students may focus on one and then another piece of information, without ever combining them into a series or synthesizing them into a whole unit of thought. Becoming aware of the need for this kind of thinking, however, can help even students with difficulties in processing information to improve. When tasks are familiar and they do much of their thinking in that situa-

tion spontaneously, students most often use Thought Integration at an effective level. Inadequate use of Thought Integration is more frequently observed when students learn something new.

Examples of Ineffective Thought Integration

❑ A student focuses on the initial consonant blend in a new word but does not pay attention to the vowel sound. When the teacher focuses the student's attention on the vowel, the student forgets the consonant blend and mispronounces the word.

❑ A student is working subtraction problems in which regrouping (borrowing) is required for some but not all problems. The student attempts to regroup in every problem or always subtracts the smaller number from the larger number even when this is incorrect.

❑ The task is to circle words that have an initial letter *c* where the *c* makes the soft *s* sound. The student circles all words that begin with a *c*.

Tips for Mediating Thought Integration

■ Encourage students to become mindful of their ability to combine sources of information.

■ Ask questions that require students to respond based on the combining of sources of information such as "How do you know when your mother is mad at you?"

■ Monitor students' awareness of need to use Thought Integration automatically and point out situations where this effective use of the Building Block improved learning.

CONNECTING EVENTS
Key Concepts
To find relationships among past, present, and future learning experiences automatically

Effective use: automatic use of Connecting Events, awareness of the need for Connecting Events, thoughtfully seeking relationships across experiences

Ineffective use: Connecting Events inconsistently, fragmented view of events, lack of awareness of need for seeking relationships across events

Effective Use of Connecting Events

❏ Understand the need for Connecting Events.

❏ Relate the present event to past and future events.

❏ Use knowledge of other events to make the present event more meaningful.

Learning involves making a series of connections while integrating new information with selected information from prior experiences. Seeking relationships is a key aspect of this process. The Building Block of Connecting Events focuses on one part of seeking relationships, the forming of relationships among events across time. (Note that Thought Integration focuses on combining pieces of information into a complete thought.) Like many other Building Blocks, Connecting Events focuses on awareness of the need to engage in this kind of thinking—to connect prior, present, and future situations.

Recognizing Ineffective Use of Connecting Events
The ineffective use of this Building Block suggests that learners believe they are able to receive information from others only, that they cannot come up with ideas on their own. As discussed in the opening section of this chapter, this belief about self-efficacy can interfere with students' use of learning strategies and seriously impair learning.

This fragmented view of events affects the learners' attitude toward learning. They see themselves as recipients rather than generators of information. This ineffective functioning is determined by and, at the same time, contributes to problems in effectively using other Building Blocks.

Connecting Events inconsistently reflects, and at the same time causes, the ineffective use of several other Building Blocks. For example, a student who does not relate something in the present situation with events in the past and future demonstrates ineffective use of the blocks of Making Comparisons and Selective Attention.

Students who have difficulty with this Building Block often display a passive attitude toward activities. They are usually reluctant to work independently and find little meaning in the learning situation. The biggest problem is that these students frequently do not transfer learning from one situation to another. Teacher-mediators need to encourage such students to connect events rather than assume they need to reteach concepts these students already know.

Examples of Ineffective Connecting Events

❑ A student has difficulty transferring newly acquired skills and knowledge to other settings.

❑ A student does not apply what he learned in one learning experience to other learning experiences.

❑ A student does not see the usefulness of learning specific skills that will enable him to do more complex tasks later.

Tips for Mediating Connecting Events

■ Encourage students to talk about how the knowledge they acquire in the present experience will be useful in other situations in the future.

■ Express appreciation for those who point out how the present event is connected to prior and future events in some way.

■ Ask questions about and encourage students to ask themselves how the present learning experience is similar to prior learning experiences.

■ Monitor group work to ensure that members use the information they possess about social skills that their group worked on in prior lessons.

Confirming the Learning Experience

The Building Blocks for confirming the learning experience are Precision and Accuracy, Space and Time Concepts, Selective Attention, and Problem Identification.

PRECISION AND ACCURACY

Key Concepts

To know there is a need to understand words and concepts and use them correctly and to seek information automatically when the need arises

Effective use: awareness of need for Precision and Accuracy, use of Precision and Accuracy automatically

Ineffective use: lack of awareness of need for Precision and Accuracy, expressing words and ideas carelessly, inadequate understanding of words and ideas

Effective Use of Precision and Accuracy

❏ Think about the need for Precision and Accuracy.

❏ Seek a precise understanding of words and concepts when needed.

❏ When communicating thoughts and actions, use words and ideas as correctly as possible.

Awareness of the need for Precision and Accuracy can help learners develop strategies that dramatically improve their effectiveness in a challenging learning experience. This Building Block is one of four that focuses on confirming the learning experience, which means to understand more completely, clarify misunderstandings, validate ideas, correct mistaken ideas, narrow the focus, and define needs. A quality control mechanism, the Precision and Accuracy Building Block helps the learner strive for excellence.

This Building Block provides the clearest example of the importance of awareness of a need. Note that awareness of need for Precision and Accuracy regarding words and concepts is not about building a large vocabulary. Rather, it focuses on the

importance of knowing when one does not know. This Building Block addresses the need for striving to know more to solve a problem.

The main idea of Precision and Accuracy is for learners to solve problems by developing a need to find out the exact meaning of concepts that confuse them (precise understanding and systematic Exploration) and to find out if they have expressed their thoughts correctly (accurate use and controlled Expression). Establishing this need can provide the value and interest a learner must have to approach a learning experience effectively and make meaning of it in a manner that leads to better thinking and learning.

This Building Block more than any other can help learners understand that learning experiences place demands on learners. As learners figure out these needs, the challenges lessen, and successful and even excellent learning can occur. Every challenging task places a demand on learners to understand its concepts clearly and to communicate very carefully their ideas related to it.

Precision and Accuracy can help students develop strategies for better communication among peoples with different personal frames of reference, or worldviews. Students gain a much deeper understanding about the need for Precision and Accuracy when they learn that even one simple idea can have a very different meaning for each member of a group based on past experiences. For example, in a group talking about camping, one person might think about backpacking, another about a lot full of recreational vehicles, another about a tent in the woods. Group members can make many assumptions about what another member says unless a precise understanding and accurate use of words becomes a need for the group (see the dialogue tips in Figure 3.5).

Recognizing Ineffective Use of Precision and Accuracy

It is important for teacher-mediators to identify students with language deficiencies and help them enlarge their receptive and expressive vocabularies. However, recognizing vocabulary development needs as a part of determining ineffective use of this Building Block is not as important as recognizing students' lack of awareness of the need for the Building Block. Students displaying this problem do not have a good strategy for overcoming an imprecise understanding. They may explore systematically to gather more information without realizing that their problem is actually inability to understand precisely the information they have already available. Such students display a similar problem with their expression of ideas. A student with a lack of need for accurate use of words and concepts may be aware that her teammates are confused by what she is telling them but act as though she has no control over the problem and no responsibility for solving the problem.

Many students display an egocentric communication problem. They act as though others know their worlds as well as they do. When they describe an event

FIGURE 3.5

Questions and Comments that Facilitate Effective Dialogue

Dialogue leads to a blending of knowledge among learners based on seeking a clear understanding of others' frames of reference for interpreting the world.

❏ Please say more about _____.

❏ What does _____ mean to you?

❏ And you think that because _____?

❏ Why do you think _____?

❏ I am a bit confused about how _____ fits with what we are studying because I see that [provide an explanation of your own thinking]. What do you think?

❏ Why did you ask that question? (Ask this of someone who has just asked a question, either before or after it is answered.)

❏ I am curious about what others are thinking. Would some of you share your thoughts?

❏ I see a relationship between what the two of you are saying. [Explain.] Would you both tell me what you think about what I've just said?

Note: even young and special needs students can engage in dialogue and questioning. Place questions on the walls of the classroom, and tell students to use these samples to help them ask good questions of others within their mediated learning community.

orally or in writing, these students are not aware that others may need more details about the event that is perfectly clear to them without these details. A lack of awareness of need for Precision and Accuracy, inadequate understanding of words and concepts, or careless use of words and concepts can cause others to think students are not capable of engaging in highly challenging learning activities. It is very important, then, to help students develop an awareness of need for Precision and Accuracy.

Examples of Ineffective Precision and Accuracy

❏ A student comments to others on a Tuesday, "Yesterday we went to Sunday School." The student does not notice the puzzled looks of the others.

❏ One student says to another: "Please get us enough paper towels for this project." The student leaves the classroom without making sure that she knows where to find the paper towels and what the student means by "enough."

❑ Team members do not question the teacher's comment: "I hope you finish your project today." Does the teacher expect the team to finish in two hours or in fifteen minutes?

❑ A student gathers very little information even though she appears to be approaching the learning experience in an organized manner.

❑ A student appears unable to follow directions.

❑ Team members do not ask for clarification of aspects of an activity.

Tips for Mediating Precision and Accuracy

■ A simple activity helps students understand the need for Precision and Accuracy in giving directions. With a loaf of bread, a jar of peanut butter, a jar of jelly, and a knife, ask students to provide directions for making a peanut butter and jelly sandwich. The sandwich maker must follow directions without making any inferences: if a student says, "Put the peanut butter on the bread," the sandwich maker places the jar of peanut butter on the bag of bread. Do this activity as a class or as a group activity with each group writing instructions and exchanging them with another group that attempts to follow the instructions. Have students provide feedback on the precision of the directions.

■ Dialogue-type questions help promote Precision and Accuracy because of the emphasis on inquiring into others' views rather than on advocacy and debate. Figure 3.5 presents a list of questions and comments that have proved helpful in exploring underlying assumptions on a range of topics.

■ Assist students in developing a precise understanding of new words and concepts that are the focus of a given lesson.

■ Help students develop a precise understanding of relationships among objects and events through the use of comparison terms, such as *same*, *opposite*, and *different*.

■ Occasionally use words students do not know. Encourage them to listen for these unfamiliar terms and ask for an explanation.

■ Establish an expectation for all class members to be appreciated when they ask for clarification.

■ On a daily basis, ask students to pose these questions to themselves and answer them precisely: "What do I really know about this concept?" and "What do I want to know about this learning experience?"

■ Model how easy it is to misunderstand what another person is trying to communicate.

■ Use accurate terms for objects and events, and expect all class members to learn the words they need to do the same.

SPACE AND TIME CONCEPTS
Key Concepts
To understand and use information about space and time that is important in almost all learning

Effective use: well-developed understanding of Space and Time Concepts, satisfactory use of Space and Time Concepts

Ineffective use: inadequate use of Space and Time Concepts, impaired use of Space and Time Concepts

Effective Use of Space and Time Concepts

❑ Relate objects according to size, shape, distance, and location.

❑ Relate objects in space to each other with an external orientation such as north, east, south, and west or an internal orientation such as front, back, right, or left.

❑ Relate objects or events according to the order in which they occur.

❑ Relate events according to how long they last or how much time occurs between particular events.

The concepts of space and time affect almost all learning. To understand arithmetic concepts, a student must understand size and order, concepts of space and time. To read a word, a student must understand cues about size and shape of letters and their spacing on the page. Learners need these concepts at a more abstract level for all learning. For example, learners can understand more deeply the effect on all living things of the destruction of rain forests when they can experience the size, the enormity, of the problem.

Time and space are relative concepts. One can view space from an internal, personal frame of reference (front, back, left, right) or from an external frame of reference (north, south, east, west) shared by everyone. One's culture defines one's concept of time and space. Some people and cultures measure and use time very precisely: modern business culture, for example, has developed very precise ways of measuring time, including values for and beliefs about punctuality, efficiency, deadlines, "time is money," and so on. Other cultures measure time in much more

vague terms and do not, for example, expect others to appear for gatherings at a set time. Time is also relative based on one's frame of reference: with good friends, time flies; in a dull class, an hour lasts forever. Teachers need to be aware that students bring their family culture's frame of reference for time to school, so they cannot expect all children to have the school's frame of reference for time. They need to understand that they must mediate time.

Culture also defines personal space, the distance appropriated to individuals in a group setting. Americans require much more personal space than people in most other cultures do; they often are surprised by how close strangers stand to them when they visit another country.

The Building Block of Space and Time differs in an important way from other Building Blocks. It is the only Block that focuses on domains, or subjects, that impact but are not limited to metastrategic knowledge. The reason Feuerstein includes impaired Space and Time Concepts in his list of cognitive deficiencies and functions (Feuerstein et al. 1980), and the reason these concepts are a part of CEA is that an understanding of Space and Time Concepts, or the lack of it, affects one's effectiveness in thinking, and development of knowledge about Space and Time Concepts depends more on mediated learning than most domains.

Recognizing Ineffective Use of Space and Time Concepts

To function in a classroom and to form relationships among ideas, students must understand such spatial concepts as the following: front, back, left, right, up, down, in, on, under, between, beside, near, through, over, around, behind, first, last, middle, far, east, south, west, and north. At a more concrete level, students need knowledge of spatial concepts to follow directions; for example, "Draw a line under the correct answer." Often problems in understanding these concepts are hidden. As a result, a teacher may assume students cannot determine the correct response rather than questioning the students' understanding of spatial directions.

Ineffectiveness in the use of time concepts is often even more hidden than problems with spatial orientation. Learners with lack of understanding of time concepts seldom refer to events in the past or future. If they mention such events, they speak of them as though they are occurring in the present or in some vague other time. Some students have difficulty determining the order in which events took place or how best to sequence events in a plan. Lack of ability to sequence and order objects and events effectively affects students' ability to see relationships among concepts or determine the main idea of relationships. Just as it is often difficult to know whether a student can tell time on a clock, it is often difficult to determine that the student has trouble with sequencing.

Cultural norms affect sequencing as well. Most indigenous peoples, for example, use a fourfold system of associating events based on the four directions. Western societies generally use a three-part system of first, second, third or beginning, middle, end. Unaware that the student's cultural understanding of time and space differs, teachers might make assumptions about the students' lack of ability to sequence parts of a story accurately when the problem is a lack of knowledge about the system.

Examples of Ineffective Space and Time Concepts

❑ A student gives vague spatial directions ("over there") when asked to explain an object's location.

❑ A student is unable to summarize a story into the requested three parts of beginning, middle, and end. Instead, two separate events are presented in an unrelated manner in the middle part such as "The boy went to the playground. The boy chased the ball. A fire engine drove past with its sirens blaring. The boy went home."

❑ Told he has five more minutes to work on his project, a student asks if he has time to start over.

❑ A student cannot justify why she estimates the number of beans in a jar as hundreds more than anyone else estimates.

❑ A student attempts to put books in a space that is too small to hold them.

❑ A student confuses terms for spatial information.

❑ A student uses gestures instead of words to explain an object's location.

Tips for Mediating Space and Time Concepts

■ Establish expectations in the classroom for students to use Space and Time Concepts precisely, and seek to expand understanding of related concepts regularly. Perhaps have students research various concepts of time and space and take turns sharing the precise and accurate use.

■ Help students find relationships among ideas, objects, and events based on time or space characteristics.

■ Ask students to explain how to use time and space in given tasks.

■ Monitor team use of time and space: observe how team members judge time as they work, and how they use space to contribute to their success such as arranging their seating to work together better.

SELECTIVE ATTENTION

Key Concepts

To choose between relevant and irrelevant information and to focus on the information needed in the learning experience

Effective use: active use of Selective Attention, adequate use of Selective Attention, well-developed Selective Attention

Ineffective use: inadequate use of select attention, partial use of Selective Attention, impaired Selective Attention

Effective Use of Selective Attention

- ❏ Decide what information is important to think about.

- ❏ Decide what information is not important to think about.

- ❏ Focus on all relevant information.

- ❏ Ignore irrelevant information.

An important aspect of effective thinking, Selective Attention focuses on the control learners can have over the information they use in a learning experience. When students are thinking and learning, they must narrow the focus from the vast amount of available stimuli as the working memory cannot focus on everything available. Information comes from memory as well as from the outside world. Many learners make selections automatically, as when they ignore the traffic noise outside of the classroom. However, not all learners find ignoring noises an automatic process!

The Building Block of Selective Attention focuses on decision making regarding what information receives attention. Some available information is relevant to the learning experience and other information is not. If the purpose of the learning experience changes, relevant information might change.

A classroom example explains how the relevance of information differs with the purpose of the learning activity. If the goal of an art project is for students to make something unique out of a given set of materials, then relevant cues include the available materials and ideas about how to use the materials in a clever and unusual manner. If, however, the goal is for students to use the materials to make table decorations that should look as much alike as possible, the relevant cues are quite different. They now need a model for the table decoration, directions on how to make the object, and attention to any changes that might occur as everyone works.

The schemas learners develop to organize information also affect Selective Attention. Schemas provide learners with a theory about some concept: a schema about the characteristics of bears might describe them as playful, intelligent, mostly vegetarian animals or as ferocious, strong beasts that attack humans. According to the schema, a person attends to different cues when meeting a bear in the forest.

Learners must maintain Selective Attention throughout the learning experience. Their ability to do so depends to a great extent on the degree to which they are oriented toward a goal. The Tool of Goal Orientation can help students use Selective Attention better. If learners put energy into striving to reach a goal, they are more motivated to attend selectively and effectively.

Recognizing Ineffective Use of Selective Attention

Learners often become distracted by irrelevant cues around them during the learning experience. Some find it easy to refocus; other learners have more difficulty, particularly when the task is complex or the learner is dealing with affective-motivational needs that interfere. Ineffective use of Selective Attention can also occur due to a lack of precise understanding of an activity's purpose or by lack of an effective use of Goal Orientation.

Impaired Selective Attention due to a focus on irrelevant cues is easy to observe. In some cases, however, the problem may have more to do with a learner's inability to decide between relevant and irrelevant information, which might lead the teacher-mediator to assume the student is incapable of completing the task.

Examples of Ineffective Selective Attention

- ❏ The class is studying a photograph of two species of elephants to determine the differences in their physical characteristics. One student comments on a hole in the corner of the photo.

- ❏ A student uses black paint in a painting of fresh apples and strawberries.

- ❏ Team members spend much of their project time talking about a class party.

- ❏ A student pays attention to the off-task behavior of a popular person in the group because he believes he will be more successful if he acts more like the other student.

- ❏ A student can't decide what book to read for a report due in three days.

- ❏ One team member is not paying attention, but the team hasn't noticed and appoints that member recorder of the work.

Tips for Mediating Selective Attention

❏ Encourage students to consider the purpose of a learning experience when they decide what information is relevant to their work.

❏ Establish expectations in the class that students justify their selection of relevant information and broaden schemas when needed.

❏ Ask questions about how Goal Orientation helps students use Selective Attention continuously ("If your goal is to finish the project today, what information is relevant to achieving that goal?").

❏ Monitor the need for Selective Attention throughout the school day, and talk with students about how to use Selective Attention to stay focused.

PROBLEM IDENTIFICATION

Key Concepts

To experience a sense of imbalance automatically and define its cause when something interferes with successful learning

Effective use: automatic use of Problem Identification, thoughtful Problem Identification

Ineffective use: inadequate use of Problem Identification, impaired Problem Identification, lack of awareness of need to use Problem Identification

Effective Use of Problem Identification

❏ Experience a sense of imbalance when a problem occurs.

❏ Define problems that are experienced.

❏ Use Problem Identification automatically.

Problem Identification focuses on experiencing and defining problems spontaneously in a learning experience. Effective learners continuously monitor the learning experience situation

Ineffective Use

Problem Identification

Effective Use

for any feeling of imbalance that indicates a need to make some kind of adjustment. For example, when a student notices others in the classroom repeatedly looking at her team with frowns on their faces, she realizes something is out of balance—her team is disrupting the work of others—and she suggests to her teammates that they work more quietly.

The second part of Problem Identification is as important as the first. Students must define the imbalance they sense to remove its cause. Experiencing and defining the problem lead to Problem Identification. To help young students understand Problem Identification, some preschool teachers changed the seating arrangement before students arrived one morning. Students were used to a routine of coming into the classroom and sitting at a particular place at the table where their names were boldly displayed on placemats. As students came to the table that particular morning, some started to sit down in their usual places and immediately experienced an imbalance as they noticed someone else's name at their place. Most were able to define the problem as "Someone else's name is on my usual seat." This led to their looking around until they found their names, then sitting in the new place. A few children experienced the problem but did not attempt to define it in a manner that helped them solve the problem: they either looked uncomfortable as they sat down in the old place, or they stood beside the table looking confused. Others sat down in their former spots without noticing the altered nameplates.

Recognizing Ineffective Use of Problem Identification

Some learners are completely unaware of the sense of imbalance that accompanies problems. This lack of awareness seems to be the case especially for interpersonal relationship problems, resulting in many difficulties for learners in the classroom and in all social situations at home and, potentially, at work. An example of lack of awareness might be a student who is making jokes during class. The teacher keeps looking at him with a frown, and although the student sees the teacher, he does not recognize her facial expression as a problem related to him.

Difficulty experiencing a problem (not sensing the imbalance that occurs) and defining a problem results from not gathering information as well as not establishing relationships among pieces of information. Teacher-mediators can observe impaired Problem Identification in learners by watching students' body language and facial expressions. If a problem exists and students display no hesitancy, no tensing of muscles or look of confusion, the teacher-mediator can assume students have not monitored the environment and are not experiencing the problem. Some students might display some sign of imbalance but not make any changes to correct the problem. They might become less actively involved in the learning experience instead, which indicates they have not been able or have not attempted to define the problem. Some students depend on others to define and solve their problems, asking for help at the slightest feeling of imbalance. While it is important for

these students to know that they are exhibiting an important part of Problem Identification, they cannot become effective independent learners unless they also learn to define the problem for themselves before seeking assistance.

Impaired Problem Identification is closely related to the ineffective use of other Building Blocks. Lack of Planning, impulsive Exploration, lack of awareness of need for Precision and Accuracy, and many other bad habits of learning can occur because learners are unaware of the need to identify problems for themselves.

Examples of Ineffective Problem Identification

- ❏ A student enters a room where two people stop yelling at each other abruptly, and the student is oblivious to the tension between the other two people.

- ❏ A child gets up from rest time, puts her right shoe on her left foot and the left shoe on her right foot, and runs off to play.

- ❏ A teacher is reading a story to a group of children. One child lays down on his back and begins to kick his feet in the air. The teacher stops reading and calls out his name. The child looks at the teacher and continues to kick his feet in the air.

- ❏ During a small-group activity, the teacher asks each student to place a blue cube on top of a red cube. One student places the red cube on top. The teacher slides her correctly placed cubes beside the student's incorrectly placed cubes and asks him to explain what is wrong with his placement. The child has difficulty seeing why his placement is incorrect.

- ❏ A student continuously questions other class members about what she is supposed to be doing.

Tips for Mediating Problem Identification

- Encourage students to describe any imbalances they experience in the classroom.

- Establish an expectation in the classroom for students to define a problem and explain their strategy for solving the problem before others help them with the problem. Assist students in defining the problem and developing a strategy as needed.

- Intentionally and routinely create problems or act in an unexpected manner to facilitate a shared experience in Problem Identification the class can analyze together. Start an activity at an unusual time of day, for example. Even actions as small as wearing sunglasses in a darkened room can lead to interesting dialogues related to Problem Identification.

- Monitor use of corrective actions teacher-mediators often use to help students overcome problems. Delay these actions until students have an opportunity to experience the problem. For example, give students time to notice a misspelled word before correcting it. (Note: Some types of problems need immediate, low-key correction such as rephrasing a student's use of poor grammar when speaking. Use judgment to determine when and how to focus attention on problems.)

- Question students about an activity's steps before responding to a request for repeated directions.

- Help students understand that problems occur in all kinds of situations and to even the most effective learners.

- Emphasize the need to gather information systematically and from more than one source when experiencing problems.

- Relate problems and explain what happened in experiencing, defining, and solving them.

Summary of Building Blocks of Thinking

CEA teacher-mediators consistently report that they develop a clear understanding of Building Blocks of Thinking only after they use the minilessons with students. Insight develops as they see the power of the Building Blocks in helping students develop strategies that make them more effective thinkers and learners. The following points summarize the most important information that applies to all the Building Blocks of Thinking.

- ❏ Only occasionally do learners use a Building Block perfectly or at a totally ineffective level. The goal is to move toward more effective use more often and to be aware of the availability of the metastrategic knowledge about the Building Blocks that helps overcome challenges in the process of learning.

❏ The less energy learners need to use a Building Block, the more effective they are. If they need more energy and time, learning is more difficult.

❏ The degree of effectiveness with which a learner uses each Building Block changes based on many factors related to the learning experience. Learners might display a highly effective level of use of a Building Block on one occasion and a much lower level on another. For example, a student may use Exploration in a highly systematic manner during a math lesson and Exploration in a highly impulsive manner during a reading lesson on the same day. The goal of teacher-mediators is to help students become aware of their ability to use Building Blocks effectively in some situations and to transfer that ability to other situations where they use the Building Block less effectively.

❏ Building Blocks work in relation to each other. Therefore, it is not a problem if teacher-mediators cannot determine exactly which Building Block would help a student most or which Building Block the student is using the least effectively at the time. It is important students receive the support they need to develop strategies that can improve learning in the given situation.

❏ Effective use of one Building Block can help learners overcome problems related to use of another Building Block. Teacher-mediators may switch focus from one Building Block to another when students have a great deal of trouble with one Building Block.

❏ The Building Blocks of Thinking are prerequisites to all thinking and are readily applied to any learning situation. Helping learners gain insight into the knowledge the Blocks provide about the process of learning gives learners a very real sense of improved self-efficacy.

❏ The Building Blocks in each of the three categories (approaching, making meaning of, and confirming the learning experience) can help students develop strategies more closely related to another of the categories. For example, Selective Attention is as helpful to learners in making meaning of a learning experience as it is in confirming a learning experience. The categories aid recall of the concepts and highlight these aspects of cognitive processing.

❏ Building Blocks focus primarily on cognitive processing; yet, the awareness of need that is the primary focus of several Building Blocks are, in part, affective-motivational factors. Affective-motivational factors impact the use of each of the Building Blocks. Understanding the relationship between Building Blocks of Thinking and affective-motivational Tools of Learning helps a learner embrace learning experiences in their true, holistic nature.

Tools of Learning

CEA's metastrategic approach strives to integrate three aspects of learning—cognition, affect, and motivation—with the Tools focusing on affective-motivational approaches. The relationship among cognition, motivation, and affect are not thoroughly understood, but there is no question that each is vitally important to the other. It may be more accurate to view them as often-overlapping dimensions of learning rather than neatly separate categories.

The Tools of Learning have been placed somewhat arbitrarily into two categories: 1. understanding feelings within the learning experience and 2. motivating behavior within the learning experience. Some Tools, such as Feeling of Competence, address both affective and motivational approaches. Affective-motivational approaches to learning are not easily defined, observed, or measured; yet, much has been learned about their effect on learning. CEA students and teacher-mediators find that these Tools lead to the development of powerful learning strategies that complete the picture of effective learning.

The discussion of each Tool mirrors the Building Blocks format, providing information on the role the Tool plays in learning, a description of its effective use, examples of ineffective use, and tips on how to mediate each Tool. Like the Building Blocks, two tips apply to mediating each Tool:

❏ Use minilessons to help students develop metastrategic knowledge about the specific Tool.

❏ Use bridging to help students develop decontextualized principles and examples of strategies related to the principles that they can use in a variety of situations where they need this specific Tool.

An explanation of the use of minilessons and bridging appears in chapter 4.

Understanding Feelings within the Learning Experience

Affect (feeling) colors every thought and energizes every action (Greenfield 1996). More specifically, feelings energize cognitive processes put into the service of meeting learners' motivational needs. The four Tools of Learning for understanding feelings are Inner Meaning, Feeling of Challenge, Awareness of Self-Change, and Feeling of Competence.

INNER MEANING

Key Concepts

To seek deep, personal value in learning experiences that energizes thinking and behavior and leads to greater commitment and success

Effective use: clear use of Inner Meaning, adequate use of Inner Meaning, personal value

Ineffective use: insufficient use of Inner Meaning, lack of personal value

Effective Use of Inner Meaning

- ❏ Find deep, personal value in the learning experience.

- ❏ Think about why the learning experience is important, interesting, and useful.

- ❏ Think about how the learning experience relates to the world outside of school.

When learners feel an experience is personally important, interesting, and useful, the potential for successful learning increases dramatically. Learners' performance on academic tasks, their persistence or Goal Orientation, their choice of continuing with the task until completion, and their use of learning strategies relates to the degree to which they value the learning experience. When the learning experience has strong intrinsic value, learners use more effective Selective Attention, Working Memory, and the other Building Blocks that assist in making meaning as well as more effective Self-Regulation. Inner Meaning is the key to energizing the need for every Building Block and Tool.

The Tool of Inner Meaning is the same as the essential quality of meaning that effective teacher-mediators use to energize mediated learning experiences (see chapter 2). CEA includes it as a Tool of Learning to emphasis the need for learners to energize learning experiences for themselves if they are to become effective independent learners.

Recognizing Ineffective Use of Inner Meaning

If they do not value academic success, students will not develop and use learning strategies. Psychological needs determine value as well as the importance the environment in which the student lives places on learning, whether society at large or close friends and family. A cultural mismatch between student and school values can have detrimental effects on Inner Meaning.

When teacher-mediators share meaning with students, the example brings power to mediated learning experiences. But students must learn to develop their own Inner Meaning. Inner Meaning heightens intrinsic value and enjoyment for the student. Extrinsic reinforcement, or rewards, may detract from the intrinsic value students might place on a learning experience. Rewards might influence school performance, but their long-term effects are questionable. Unlike Inner Meaning, they do not lead as clearly to effective independent learning. Students who find Inner Meaning in learning situations do not need extrinsic reinforcement.

Examples of Ineffective Inner Meaning

❏ A student wants to start a new project when experiencing a problem on the current one.

❏ A student is preoccupied by the grade she thinks she will receive for her work instead of seeing the task as a valuable learning experience.

❏ Students look bored and frustrated as they begin to work on a group project.

❏ Students cannot decide what books they want to read.

Tips for Mediating Inner Meaning

■ Encourage students to share with the class what makes learning important, interesting, and useful to them.

■ Ask questions that help students explore why it is important to find Inner Meaning in learning experiences such as "Why do you want to learn about this subject?"

■ Give students the opportunity to reflect on Inner Meaning such as through journal writing.

■ When a student does not want to do a task, help him find some aspect of the task that excites him and adapt the task to meet his needs better.

■ Create activities that relate to students' real-world needs. Encourage students to discuss how various tasks meet this standard.

FEELING OF CHALLENGE

Key Concepts

To energize learning in new and complex experiences by focusing on the learning process rather than fear and anxiety about a possible unsuccessful product

Effective use: appropriate management of Feeling of Challenge

Ineffective use: ineffective management of Feeling of Challenge

Effective Use of Feeling of Challenge

❏ Become aware of any positive or negative feelings of challenge and any behaviors that help avoid the learning experience.

❏ Focus more attention on positive feelings about commitment to the learning process and less attention on fear and anxiety about the possibility of a failed product.

❏ Break down complex learning experiences into manageable parts.

❏ Ease anxiety by focusing on parts of a challenging learning experience that are familiar.

The degree to which learning experiences challenge learners is based on how novel (containing many new concepts or tasks) the learning experience is and how complex (containing numerous parts). Novelty and complexity are relative to each learner's perceptions, past experiences, and understanding of the subject matter. Teacher-mediators cannot always predict how much a learning experience will challenge students. The goal in CEA classrooms is for learners to engage in challenging learning experiences as often as possible. A learner cannot become effective at an independent level without learning to deal with challenges. Challenge can be viewed from a positive or negative perspective. Use of the Tool of Feeling of Challenge is essential for students who experience more anxiety than is beneficial. According to research concerning achievement-related values as reported by Wigfield (1994), negative emotions of anxiety and fear relate to students' beliefs about the possibility of failure and success and the effort they need to engage in the learning experience.

Some learners need support and encouragement to learn how to control their negative feelings and to develop strategies to help them be successful with challenging tasks. Teachers can provide some of this support. Students can achieve more success, however, when they work in collaborative and cooperative teams. An anxious student finds it highly therapeutic when peers dealing with the same difficulties and those who can facilitate mediated learning experiences join the student in tackling a challenging experience. In this manner, students can help each other avoid adopting self-defeating strategies. Perhaps the most important way for students to manage negative feelings of challenge is to learn to focus more on positive feelings about their commitment to the learning process and less on fear and anxiety about the possibility of failure. In a laboratory for learning, which focuses on these techniques, Feeling of Challenge is mediated most of the time.

Recognizing Ineffective Use of Feeling of Challenge

Garcia and Pintrich (1994) describe common counterproductive strategies for dealing with challenge. Self-handicapping involves the creation of obstacles for oneself to maintain a feeling of self-worth and positive self-schemas (beliefs); for example, a student announces that she has carpal tunnel syndrome so she can say that she could create a good presentation if typing wasn't so painful. Underachieving, or deliberately exerting minimal effort, is a kind of self-handicapping. It provides an opportunity to look good, at least to oneself, because if success occurs, it is based on little effort, which supports the belief that one has a high level of ability. If failure occurs, the minimal effort expended provides an excuse and protects the person's sense of self-worth. Students who employ a self-handicapping strategy wait until very late to begin an assignment or take on too many tasks at one time.

Another counterproductive strategy is defensive pessimism. One sets unrealistically low expectations for oneself to control anxiety, prepare for failure, and motivate oneself to exert a lot of effort to avoid failure. The student who believes she has failed an exam yet does better than most others engages in this strategy.

While counterproductive strategies help one avoid engaging in a task for fear of failure, reactive strategies occur after the failure has occurred. One reactive strategy is self-affirmation. A student may use this strategy in reaction to a negative evaluation of his performance in an area where the student had considered himself a good learner. The student seeks to reaffirm his self-concept by avoiding the challenging subject matter and engaging in activities that lead to a positive evaluation from others.

A student does not have to have learning problems to fear challenge. In fact, many academically gifted students fear challenge more than most others because they have little opportunity to learn how to deal with it. When faced with something that is appropriately challenging for them, they often engage in a counterproductive strategy.

For students to confront negative feelings and enjoy challenges, they need to understand how negative feelings become associated with challenge. Most people fear the unknown—the novelty aspect of challenge. The complexity of challenging experiences can make them appear more difficult than they really are. Familiarity with the topic can overcome the fear, and breaking the task into smaller parts can lessen its complexity. When students develop strategies for dealing with novelty and complexity, challenging tasks can become fun and even exciting.

A supportive learning environment that values process more than product can also help students overcome negative feelings of challenge. When the classroom is a place to explore and overcome challenges, the negative feelings toward challenge often dissipate. In contrast, students feel much more anxious in a challenging situation if they think the classroom community will judge them solely on their product in the task rather than appreciate them for applying Building Blocks and Tools in effective learning, which may or may not result in the right answer.

Effective independent learners thrive on challenge. It is difficult to become an independent learner unless one learns to deal effectively with Feeling of Challenge.

Examples of Ineffective Feeling of Challenge

- ❏ A student waits until the night before a major project is due to get started.

- ❏ A student sets goals that are unrealistically low for her ability.

- ❏ A student finds reasons to leave the classroom whenever he is expected to write responses to questions.

- ❏ A student is overly worried about taking a test.

Tips for Mediating Feeling of Challenge

- ■ Encourage students to share their feelings of fear and anxiety regarding challenge, and work on developing strategies together for gaining a positive Feeling of Challenge.

- ■ Present many challenging activities in a nonthreatening environment where support is available.

- ■ Help students understand that it is important to tackle challenging activities even if they are unsuccessful at first. Give feedback on the learning process rather than on the final product.

- ■ Establish expectations that students exert an appropriate amount of effort when engaged in challenging tasks, and allow them to seek help from others to develop strategies for overcoming problems.

AWARENESS OF SELF-CHANGE
Key Concepts
To recognize and understand feelings related to personal growth and to learn to expect and welcome change and development

Effective use: appropriate use of Awareness of Self-Change

Ineffective use: inappropriate use of Awareness of Self-Change

Effective Use of Awareness of Self-Change

❑ Become aware of being a person who changes and develops.

❑ Become aware of feelings related to changing and developing.

❑ Learn to expect and welcome change and development.

Everyone experiences change, and learners need to be aware of themselves as changing and developing. Becoming aware of self-change can impact learning in negative and positive ways. Negative reactions occur when learners are uncomfortable with the change that has occurred because it changes their beliefs about themselves. Positive reactions occur when learners become impressed with their ability to develop new skills.

The focus of this Tool of Learning is awareness of change taking place within oneself, to expect it and to welcome it. Appropriate understanding of Awareness of Self-Change can help students overcome an inadequate Feeling of Competence and deal with a Feeling of Challenge. When students recognize they have changed and will continue to change, they fear challenges less because they realize they are capable of changing and, thus, of having success in challenging situations. They know past failures do not mean competence is unattainable.

Learners need to understand the value and universality of change. They also need to know that change comes from within each person. Everyone is responsible for changes necessary for them to become effective learners.

Recognizing Ineffective Use of Awareness of Self-Change

Some people resist change. They prefer to remain in their comfort zone. When learners who were having major learning problems begin to improve in noticeable ways, teacher-mediators need to help them expect and welcome self-change. For example, a student who is beginning to make real improvement in literacy skills might actually stop trying as hard because it would mean others would expect her to continue to make dramatic progress. She might feel uncomfortable with the way she is changing. People are most concerned about their relationships with others as they change. If a student improves in reading, she might join a new reading group, leave old friends behind, and be anxious about whether the new group will accept her. The student needs help understanding that she is still the same person in many ways, just one who has developed new abilities in the area of literacy.

Examples of Ineffective Awareness of Self-Change

- ❑ A student appears anxious rather than excited when the teacher-mediator tells him how much his writing has improved.

- ❑ A student is moved from a group of lower functioning students in reading to a higher group and starts to regress.

- ❑ A student is angry when told she no longer needs extra help for reading.

Tips for Mediating Awareness of Self-Change

- ■ Encourage students to observe self-change by keeping notebooks that show progress on given skills. Discuss how much students have learned, and compare their performance now with their past performance.

- ■ Establish expectations in the classroom for celebrating major changes in individual students and valuing this process.

- ■ Ask questions to determine how students feel about self-change. Make it acceptable for everyone to talk openly about these feelings.

- ■ Monitor team change and encourage team members to appreciate the group's positive changes.

FEELING OF COMPETENCE

Key Concepts

To energize feelings, thoughts, and behavior by developing beliefs about being capable of learning and doing something effectively

Effective use: well-developed Feeling of Competence

Ineffective use: inadequate Feeling of Competence

Effective Use of Feeling of Competence

❑ Become aware of secure and insecure feelings about the ability to learn and do something effectively.

❑ Look for reasons to support a personal belief in ability to learn and do something effectively.

❑ Overcome feelings of self-doubt that prevent belief in personal abilities.

❑ Understand the importance of developing a Feeling of Competence and its ability to energize feelings, thoughts, and behaviors.

A Feeling of Competence may well be the most important Tool of Learning combines affective and motivational factors in powerful ways. Teachers helping students develop a Feeling of Competence must do so carefully. When they observe students' frustration with learning activities that are too difficult, some may provide activities that offer little challenge. This practice, however, often leads to students experiencing an even less adequate Feeling of Competence. Students need positive stress and challenge to develop Feeling of Competence. Even low functioning learners are affected negatively when tasks are too easy for them. Learners with a positive Feeling of Competence use more effective learning strategies.

Beliefs about oneself, or self-schemas, play an important role in one's effectiveness in feeling competent. People's experiences produce self-schemas. The more accurate the self-schemas of past, present, and predicted future, the more individuals can build a Feeling of Competence when it is not adequate in a given situation.

Recognizing Ineffective Use of Feeling of Competence

Almost no one tries to learn something if he believes he is incapable of learning it. Emotions energize the motivation to avoid or approach learning experiences. Negative emotions protect learners by leading to the use of counterproductive strategies such as learned helplessness (see Feeling of Challenge) or lazy behavior. Students find it easier on their self-esteem to fail because they did not try than to try and fail. Many people who believe they cannot learn very well develop inaccurate self-schemas. Feeling competent is not the same as being competent. Many students who lack a Feeling of Competence do not accept their successful performance as evidence of their competence. They may need continuous feedback to develop a Feeling of Competence.

Examples of Ineffective Feeling of Competence

- ❏ A student who has just been told his work is a great improvement over past performance says, "But I am just no good at doing this!"

- ❏ A student begins to cry and is afraid to begin work on a new project.

- ❏ A student who loves to perform does not audition for the school play.

Tips for Mediating Feeling of Competence

- ■ **Give students descriptive feedback instead of isolated praise; for example, instead of saying, "Great job!" say, "I really like the way you used Exploration systematically to help you gather all the information you needed." When students have not been successful with a task, stress that they can succeed in the future based on the development and use of sound learning strategies. Before the learning experience ends, help students demonstrate some kind of success, no matter how small.**

- ■ **Establish expectations for all students to provide each other with descriptive feedback related to the process of learning with minimal praise comments that focus solely on the product.**

- ■ **Ask questions that elicit students' beliefs about themselves regarding a Feeling of Competence in an area of challenge.**

- ■ **Monitor team members' ability to mediate Feeling of Competence with each other.**

Motivating Behavior within the Learning Experience

The next four Tools of Learning focus on motivational needs and effective learning. Motivation is "a force that energizes, sustains, and directs behavior" (Eggen and Kauchak 1997, 341).

SELF-REGULATION
Key Concepts
To reflect on thoughts and actions as they occur to energize, sustain, and direct behavior toward successful learning and doing

Effective use: well-developed use of Self-Regulation

Ineffective use: inadequate use of Self-Regulation

Effective Use of Self-Regulation

❑ Reflect on thoughts and actions as they occur.

❑ Change thoughts and actions based on lessons learned from use of Self-Regulation.

❑ Use Self-Regulation to determine what Building Blocks and Tools will help develop needed learning strategies.

❑ Regulate how fast or slow to work based on how complex, how familiar, and how much time is needed to achieve success in the learning experience.

Self-Regulation focuses on the motivation to use learning strategies actively and the awareness of the use of these strategies. It also involves learners' mindfulness of their thinking and learning while they are occurring. Self-Regulation is about learners taking charge of their own learning.

Using Self-Regulation is like sitting on one's own shoulder, monitoring what one thinks and does. When using Self-Regulation effectively, students pay attention to such factors as 1. familiarity (how well they understand the task), 2. complexity (how many parts the task involves), and 3. the modality of the task (whether it

involves words, figures, numbers, etc., and the ease with which they work in that modality). Self-Regulation also involves determining the speed and direction of thinking and learning. What is an appropriate speed? Is the task moving more slowly than necessary or too quickly to ensure success? Have I gathered enough information and planned adequately?

Most teachers feel the learning situation is under better control when they regulate student behavior than when students are responsible for monitoring their own cognitive, affective, and motivational behaviors. But for students to use Self-Regulation effectively, they must take charge of their own thinking and working through tasks independently or in an appropriate interdependent manner. Teachers need not throw out established rules, especially those that help students function in a group setting, but they need to stop themselves from telling students exactly how to approach a task. They need to encourage students to think about what they are doing, what they need to do next, whether they truly need help, and how to ask for help. They must encourage students who have difficulty getting started to think about whether they are ready to begin a task and accept responsibility for doing so.

McCombs (1989) builds a strong case for putting the "self" into the theory of Self-Regulation. She recommends including a focus on self-schemas and including meaningfulness as major influences on one's effectiveness in using Self-Regulation. Self-Regulation is a powerful tool for self-monitoring of cognitive processes. It is critically important to combine it with Building Blocks related to approaching a learning experience. Learners can engage in effective systematic Exploration and Planning, for example, yet be unsuccessful in the learning experience because they did not monitor the need to make a new plan when problems occurred.

Self-Regulation relies heavily on metacognition—thinking about thinking. Many students are unaware that they are capable of reflecting on their thoughts and actions as they occur, even if they engage in this form of metacognition subconsciously. An excellent method for helping students understand and use metacognition is to have each of them complete a KWL chart stating "What I know now," "What I want to know," and "What I learned" (Ogle 1986). When learners can see what they do and do not know, they can begin to use Self-Regulation effectively. They also understand the importance of determining for themselves how to go about a task and when they have the need to develop a learning strategy.

Recognizing Ineffective Use of Self-Regulation

When students do not use Self-Regulation effectively, even the most effective use of other Building Blocks and Tools will not lead to success, at least in challenging activities. When students cannot adjust their plan when it is not working well, do not realize the need to gather more information, and do not monitor their involvement in collaborative learning, they display ineffective use of Self-Regulation. All of the Building Blocks that require continuous, spontaneous use for effective learning depend on Self-Regulation for adequate use. Without reflecting on thoughts and actions, students do not make comparisons, get the main idea, connect events, or strive to understand words and concepts and use them correctly.

Examples of Ineffective Self-Regulation

❑ A student acts impulsively, gets in trouble, and feels helpless to control his behavior.

❑ A student works slowly, pausing frequently to look out the window, even after the teacher reminds the class the assignment is due shortly.

❑ A student hurries through the assignment even though she knows it is complex and needs careful attention to detail.

Tips for Mediating Self-Regulation

■ Encourage students to share examples with the class of how they think about what they are doing while they are doing it.

■ Provide personal examples of use of Self-Regulation.

■ Establish expectations for students to accept responsibility for determining when they need help and seeking it appropriately. For example, ask students several times a week, "Who is responsible for determining when you need help? What are appropriate ways to seek help? What does this have to do with Self-Regulation?"

■ Monitor the tendency to regulate student behavior and the tendency to focus Self-Regulation on controlling acting-out behaviors instead of thinking about thinking.

GOAL ORIENTATION

Key Concepts

To take purposeful action in consistently setting, seeking, and reaching personal objectives

Effective use: active use of Goal Orientation

Ineffective use: inadequate use of Goal Orientation

Effective Use of Goal Orientation

❑ Set personally important goals.

❑ Persist in using a plan to work toward goals.

❑ Become energized by really trying to reach goals.

The Tool of Goal Orientation focuses on learners' use of motivation to lead them to action and to fulfill their intention. It involves three phases: setting a goal, persisting in behaviors necessary to attain the goal, and reaching the goal.

Effective use of Goal Orientation depends on effective use of other Tools and Building Blocks. It is closely connected to Self-Regulation in that learners must think about working toward a goal while persisting in actions to this end. Inner Meaning is also very important for successful Goal Orientation as the values learners establish energize the motivation to seek, strive for, and reach goals. Selective Attention is important for choosing the goal then controlling distractions from reaching the goal. To establish appropriate action for reaching a goal, use of all three Building Blocks for approaching a learning experience is necessary. The four Building Blocks for making meaning can assist the learner in better understanding various aspects of the goal. Without Building Blocks for confirming the learning experience, the learner may become frustrated and abandon goal-directed behavior.

The more intense the Inner Meaning for the goal, the more driven learners are to persist in goal-related behaviors. Learners must be able to answer a resounding "yes" to the question, "Do I want to succeed at this goal?" Unfortunately, many students live in a world of instant gratification where society places little emphasis on goal-directed behavior. These students need to learn that goals are worth hard work, and feelings of accomplishment are usually in direct proportion to the degree of effort. Some learners may not understand the concept of setting goals. Almost all students can benefit from reflection on the need for strategies to help them engage in effective Goal Orientation.

As with Self-Regulation, some teachers provide too many goals for students rather than encouraging them to set and seek their own goals. Effective teacher-mediators have students select a goal for themselves. One teacher-mediator reported the meaningful experience that occurred in her classroom when students set goals for their performance on projects. The emphasis was on the process for achieving goals as students established the grade they would like to receive on the project then figured out what they needed to do to succeed. Inner Meaning became much stronger for these students as did their focus on striving for excellence through the use of personal learning strategies.

Independent learning cannot take place unless learners set goals and work toward them. Interdependent learning also depends on each individual's goal-directed behavior. Collaborative learning groups can also set goals as a group and plan group strategies for seeking and reaching them.

It is important that students learn how to evaluate selected goals for feasibility. Developing a plan for reaching the goal and predicting the amount of time they need to achieve it can help students determine the feasibility. Teacher-mediators need to encourage students to set challenging goals, including ones that appear difficult to reach. If the Inner Meaning and value for the goal is strong, it might be much more feasible than seems possible initially. Some students, of course, will need support to take the risk of setting challenging goals. Team projects can really help these students take such risks more readily.

When students reach their goals, celebrating the event is important. It shows the respect of the learning community for students' persistent and strong effort. It is most important, however, that students reflect on their experience in setting, seeking, and reaching the goals. Any kind of extrinsic reward can detract from this reflection. The powerful sense of accomplishment within oneself, the resulting improved self-schemas and feelings of self-worth, are much richer results of reaching goals than any form of extrinsic reward.

Recognizing Ineffective Use of Goal Orientation

Some students have difficulty setting goals and even understanding the concept of a goal. When teachers observe little purposeful behavior unless teacher-directed, this may be the reason. However, many more students display an ineffective use of Goal Orientation after they have set goals. The problem occurs in their lack of persistence in working toward goals. These students may be very excited initially by the goal, but once they realize that reaching the goal requires hard work, their enthusiasm disappears.

With all the instant gratification available in the modern world, it can be difficult for students to learn persistence and patience with the time and effort required to reach a goal. Students need help understanding that persistence is a very important quality to develop. To do so, however, involves overcoming sometimes-strong feelings of disappointment that the goal is not easy to reach. To avoid negative feelings, some students lower their standards for the goal. Others just give up.

Examples of Ineffective Goal Orientation

❏ A student does not engage in purposeful activity during free time in the classroom.

❏ A student gets angry and quits trying when success does not come easily.

❏ A student feels frustrated when others are successful at something she has not yet mastered, but she does not see a need to set a goal related to the task.

Tips for Mediating Goal Orientation

■ Encourage students to select personal goals and evaluate their feasibility.

■ Ask questions and encourage students to ask questions that help them reflect on their goals. Use questions that facilitate dialogue (see **Precision and Accuracy**).

■ Share personal goals with the class: explain the reason for establishing those particular goals and the plan in use to reach them.

■ When students accomplish goals, hold a class ceremony. Include a special time in the ceremony for students to share strategies that helped them accomplish the goal.

■ Monitor goals set by individuals and teams. Help the students refine their strategies for engaging in more effective goal-directed behavior as needed.

■ Establish expectations for setting goals that are challenging and involve risk-taking.

SELF-DEVELOPMENT
Key Concepts
To appreciate special qualities in everyone and to enhance personal potential

Effective use: active use of Self-Development

Ineffective use: inadequate use of Self-Development

Effective Use of Self-Development

- ❏ Think about personal strengths one values, and set, seek and reach goals related to them.

- ❏ Determine personal weaknesses that interfere with developing strengths and set, seek, and reach goals related to them.

- ❏ Learn to appreciate the special qualities of others and encourage their Self-Development.

Self-Development is closely related to self-actualization, Inner Meaning, Goal Orientation, and the impact of self-schemas. It focuses on the strongly felt need in individuals to find and fulfill a purpose for their lives and to value the unique qualities or gifts they bring to the world.

Self-Development depends on understanding that one is unique and developing self-schemas that distinguish oneself from others; yet, learners who effectively use Self-Development to engage in self-actualizing behaviors feel more connected to others. People can connect with others only when they have something to contribute. These learners have been motivated to become effective independent learners to reach their goals, and they become better interdependent learners as a result.

To effectively mediate Self-Development in the classroom, teacher-mediators need to build an atmosphere that values differences among students. The class needs to celebrate differences in aptitude, learning styles, interests, worldview, and ethnicity. Students need to develop an understanding of the benefits that come from the diversity among them, which can lead to a better understanding of each other that fuels Self-Development and interdependent learning.

People's approaches to learning vary in part because their past experiences, their use of language, their self-schemas, and their personal worldviews are different.

Teacher-mediators can focus on several different goals when mediating Self-Development. One goal is to help students view themselves as active participants in a learning situation, capable of thinking and learning separately and perhaps differently from others—even the teacher. Another goal is to help students understand the unique contribution each person brings to a learning situation and, consequently, accept and appreciate these differences. Yet another goal is to help students reflect on who they think they are and what they can do to achieve their potential.

Please note that this is not a recommendation to allow students to avoid developing skills in areas where they are not strong. As a part of refining their strengths, students need to build weaker areas. Many CEA students have written in their journals that they are setting goals to work on areas in which they are weak so they can reach their overall goals for Self-Development, for being all they can be. For example, a student who values her ability to draw might set goals for improving her weaknesses in math because math skills may be very important to her goal of becoming an architect.

Recognizing Ineffective Use of Self-Development

Students with an ineffective use of Self-Development do not appreciate their unique strengths. They often express a desire to be more like someone else. They need help to see that others value their special qualities. They need help to see that they can contribute something to the group that no one else can contribute.

Students with ineffective Self-Development are unable to describe their special qualities. They also do not understand the need to assess their abilities and determine areas in which they want to develop skills. They will not set and work toward goals to develop themselves more fully.

Self-Development presents a problem for students who are marginalized in school due to cultural difference, disability, underachievement, different first language, or nontraditional learning needs. These students often hide their interest in Self-Development because they are aware of the lack of value others hold for their culture or personal worldview. As a result, these students feel ashamed and hold back from sharing with others. They also hold back from using Self-Development. As they hold back, others see them as shy, lazy, passive, and noncaring learners.

Examples of Ineffective Self-Development

❑ A student is reluctant to share what she likes to do best.

❑ A student does not initiate goal-setting related to building personal capacity.

❑ A student is frustrated because he is not good at sports and sees no value in his artistic talent.

❑ A student feels isolated from others in the classroom because she is not an extrovert.

❑ A student is reluctant to share activities from her culture with other students.

Tips for Mediating Self-Development

■ Encourage students to set goals for themselves to nurture Self-Development.

■ Establish expectations in the classroom for valuing diversity, celebrating it, and using it in ways that allow everyone to contribute their strengths.

■ Ask questions to help students explore their self-schemas, their thoughts about what they can do or would like to do.

■ Monitor teams to determine if they are organizing themselves to take advantage of each member's strengths. At the same time, ensure that students have the opportunity to be responsible for some part of group work where they will need to improve skills to contribute effectively.

■ Use bridging as a means for sharing cultural knowledge and ways of doing that reveal a student's individuality.

SHARING BEHAVIOR

Key Concepts

To energize life and learning for everyone by sharing thoughts and actions through effective interdependent learning skills

Effective use: active use of Sharing Behavior

Ineffective use: inadequate use of Sharing Behavior

Effective Sharing Behavior

- ❏ Share thoughts and actions through effective interdependent learning skills.

- ❏ Contribute to the learning of the group as a peer mediator of learning experiences and as an active learner.

- ❏ Listen to others, ask questions to understand better, and learn together.

- ❏ Use self-talk to improve learning when alone.

In a classroom that truly maximizes learning, learners need the opportunity to develop and use the Tool of Sharing Behavior. It is only through sharing thoughts among students and the teacher-mediator that class members can create a "joint-culture" (Bruner 1982) in the classroom. Joint-culture means developing shared frames of reference. Developing joint-culture is crucial if students are to pull together the Building Blocks and Tools needed to 1. develop an understanding of the formal concepts presented in classroom lessons, 2. understand the importance of the concepts they are expected to learn, and 3. develop an understanding of the significance of the goal they gain if they invest enough effort to understand the concepts (Henderson and Cunningham 1994).

Use of effective Sharing Behavior underlies the development of a laboratory for learning in the classroom and the collaborative learning that can take place in this kind of environment. Collaborative learning involves the engagement of every student as well as the teacher-mediator in conversations together where each person actively listens to others, adds meaning to what each learner/mediator shares and gives this meaning back to the group. It differs from cooperative learning in that its focus is how people create new knowledge together while cooperative learning focuses on how individuals learn as a part of a team. Cooperative and collaborative learning can certainly occur together. Unfortunately, many cooperative learning methods do not focus enough attention on the importance of collaborative learning. It is important that every member of the class accept responsibility for sharing as learners and as mediators. Sharing nurtures interdependent learning. To become an effective interdependent learner, students need to use the Tool of Sharing Behavior effectively.

Sharing Behavior underlies students' ability to participate actively in challenging, inquiry, collaborative and cooperative activities where mediated learning experiences nurture the development of metastrategic knowledge and achievement of school- and community-determined objectives for subject matter achievement. Sharing Behavior also plays an important role in learning about oneself. It is only through sharing of themselves that people come to know who they really are.

The need to share thoughts motivates learners to use Building Blocks of Thinking more effectively. For example, it creates a need for learners to use Precision and Accuracy more effectively in communicating ideas and provides a need for Selective Attention as they determine what is relevant to the conversation. It influences the way they use all the Building Blocks when approaching, making meaning of, and confirming the learning experience.

Sharing Behavior interacts with other Tools of Learning. Effective use of the Tool of Sharing Behavior depends on a Feeling of Competence and acceptance of a Feeling of Challenge. It can enhance Inner Meaning, and, according to sociocultural theories of development, it is critical to the development of Self-Regulation. It is only through effective use of Sharing Behavior that students can become effective in Self-Development.

Sharing Behavior also contributes to development when one uses it privately to verbalize strategies to oneself. Henderson and Cunningham (1994) describe its importance in internalizing and appropriating ideas and regulating one's own behavior. For example, it helps to talk to oneself about the steps involved in completing a task, out loud or silently, as a means of sharing information with oneself that otherwise might not become explicit. Learners can also use Sharing Behavior privately while reading to ask themselves questions about what is happening or to predict what will happen in the story.

Recognizing Ineffective Use of Sharing Behavior

Students, especially those who have been unsuccessful in learning in the past, may need help recognizing the need for Sharing Behavior. They may believe they do not have any ideas or skills worth contributing to the group. They may expect others to transmit knowledge to them and lack an understanding of the need to interact actively with others. As a result, these students act in a passive manner and do not contribute their thoughts and actions to an appropriate degree during group work.

Students who display inadequate use of Sharing Behavior often display inappropriate social skills. Because of their lack of value for sharing, they act in ways that show little respect for the sharing of others or for their own sharing. These students often deal with conflicts in inappropriate ways. They advocate their own ideas more than they inquire into others' ideas. They do not serve as mediators for their peers.

Examples of Ineffective Sharing Behavior

- ❏ A student sits quietly and does not share thoughts and actions with the group.

- ❏ A student does more sharing than most of her group members.

- ❏ A student does not listen to what others are sharing and changes the subject by advocating her ideas rather than inquiring into the ideas of others.

Tips for Mediating Sharing Behavior

- ■ Encourage students to engage in Sharing Behavior as learners and mediators. Demonstrate how to do this effectively.

- ■ Establish an expectation in the classroom for mediated learning experiences in which conversations flow openly among learners and the teacher-mediator.

- ■ Reduce the frequency of use of a teacher-centered approach in which students listen as information is supposedly transmitted to them and respond to mostly recall level questions. Use many more activities appropriate in a laboratory for learning.

- ■ Ask questions and help students ask questions that further the use of Sharing Behavior. Put sample questions up in the classroom for everyone to use as models (see the dialogue-facilitating questions in the section on Precision and Accuracy). The goal is to help students make meaning of concepts within the conversation as they listen to each other, add their own meanings, and explore ways to develop strategies that lead to more effective interdependent and independent learning.

Summary of Tools of Learning

The Tools of Learning have a powerful effect on helping students learn how to learn. As with the Building Blocks of Thinking, a clear understanding of the Tools comes after teachers use the minilessons with students. Insight develops as they see the power of the Tools in energizing learning. Students can develop strategies for use in specific situations to help them become more effective independent and interdependent learners. While it is very easy for teacher-mediators to use the Tools to help students rather than helping students develop an awareness of the need for the Tools, it is very important that students use Tools for themselves. The following points summarize the most important information that applies to all the Tools of Learning:

❑ Students use the Tools of Learning more or less effectively, just as they do with Building Blocks of Thinking. It is important to help students understand their effective and ineffective use.

❑ Tools share a close relationship with each other and the Building Blocks of Thinking. It is very important to help students understand these relationships and the effect Tools have on cognitive processes and other affective-motivational approaches to learning.

❑ The Tools are placed somewhat arbitrarily into the two categories of affect and motivation. Each Tool is described in terms of its contributions to 1. optimizing the positive effect of emotions that accompany thoughts and actions and impact values, or 2. motivating behavior by choosing, initiating, and persisting in specific actions as guided by one's beliefs about personal ability, desires, and values.

❑ The Tools play a powerful role in the development of effective independent and interdependent learning skills. Effective interdependent learning depends on effective independent learning, and interdependent learning can facilitate the development of independent skills.

❑ The Tools often bring metastrategic knowledge to life for learners. They touch individuals at a deep level and make them aware of the interconnectedness of cognition, affect, and motivation in all learning.

Figures 3.6 presents a reminder of the Building Blocks of Thinking along with the icons for each Building Block. Figure 3.7 lists the Tools of Learning and presents the Tool icons. Also see the Appendix for icons to display in the classroom or photocopy for individual student use.

FIGURE 3.6

CEA Building Blocks of Thinking

Building Blocks for *Approaching the Learning Experience*

 Exploration

 Planning

 Expression

Building Blocks for *Making Meaning of the Learning Experience*

 Working Memory

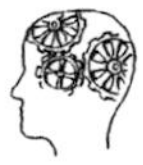

 Making Comparisons

 Getting the Main Idea

 Thought Integration

 Connecting Events

Building Blocks for *Confirming the Learning Experience*

 Precision and Accuracy

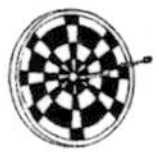

 Space and Time Concepts

 Selective Attention

 Problem Identification

FIGURE 3.7

CEA Tools of Learning

Tools for *Understanding Feelings within the Learning Experience*

 Inner Meaning

 Feeling of Challenge

 Awareness of Self-Change

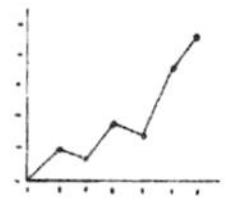

 Feeling of Competence

Tools for *Motivating Behavior within the Learning Experience*

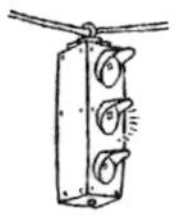

 Self-Regulation

 Goal Orientation

 Self-Development

 Sharing Behavior

Chapter 4

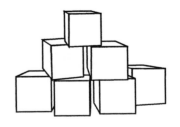

INTEGRATING
METASTRATEGIC
KNOWLEDGE INTO
THE SCHOOL
CURRICULUM

Introducing the Class to Building Blocks and Tools

For most teacher-mediators, initial integration of metastrategic knowledge into day-to-day classroom activities takes careful planning, especially if development of a more open classroom atmosphere also needs time and attention. Cognitive Enrichment Advantage (CEA) provides assistance in the form of icons with labels teachers can display in the classroom that serve as a memory aid for students and teachers learning the Building Blocks and Tools (see Appendix). (Teachers can also photocopy the icons and place them in individual booklets for students to use as a reference in any situation.) The Lesson Planning Guide that appears later in this chapter describes the steps for integrating Building Blocks and Tools into a classroom activity. The most in-depth assistance, however, is in the form of minilessons that teachers integrate into the regular curriculum and classroom activities.

CEA Minilessons

When used with the technique of bridging, which encourages the transfer of learning in one setting to other settings, minilessons help teacher-mediators integrate metastrategic knowledge into all kinds of learning activities that occur in the school setting. In this manner, activities become high quality mediated learning experiences where students gain insight into the need for Building Blocks of Thinking, Tools of Learning, and more general aspects of learning to learn. (See sample minilesson, Figure 4.1.) In *The Cognitive Enrichment Advantage Minilessons,* CEA provides 229 minilessons, 8 for each Building Block of Thinking and Tool for Learning (with the exception of the Building Block of Space and Time Concepts, which has 8 for space and 8 for time), 32 that combine two or more Building Blocks and Tools, and 28 that focus on more general aspects of learning how to learn.

When teachers use the complete set of minilessons over several months, students can develop a broad-based understanding of cognitive processes and affective-motivational approaches to learning, a shared vocabulary of metastrategic knowledge needed to construct personal learning strategies, and a general understanding of various factors involved in learning to learn. When they integrate minilessons into regular lessons, teacher-mediators help students develop and analyze personal learning strategies based on Building Blocks and Tools.

The minilessons are also an important part of teachers' professional development related to CEA. They help teacher-mediators experiment with the information in *The Cognitive Enrichment Advantage Teacher Handbook* and determine how this information fits into their personal theories of learning to learn.

A sample minilesson appears in Figure 4.1, and a description of the components of a minilesson appears in Figure 4.2. Each minilesson contains the three qualities necessary for mediated learning to occur: Intent, Meaning, and Transcendence. The

fourth essential quality, reciprocity, is not written into minilessons as the factors that determine this quality relate personally to the mediators and students involved.

FIGURE 4.1

Sample Minilesson

Selective Attention   #5

Integrate into independent activities

MEANING: Do you remember our discussion of the Building Block of Selective Attention yesterday? To search your book for information that you need, you can use Selective Attention to find your answers. Based on what you know about Selective Attention, how would you use it to find the answers to these questions? First, look in the place where you expect to find the answer. Don't look at everything. Focus on just the relevant information. If the information you need isn't there, skip to the next section, and focus your attention again.

> **INTENT:** to teach students that every effective learner needs to know how to use Selective Attention to find the answer to a specific question

TRANSCENDENCE: If I use Selective Attention to focus on what is relevant in the situation, then I will become a more effective independent learner.

FIGURE 4.2

Minilesson Components

All minilessons follow the same format.

- ❑ **Name of Building Block, Tool,** or general aspect of learning on which the minilesson focuses

- ❑ **Plan number.** The presentation order of the minilessons may prove helpful, especially to teachers implementing CEA for the first time; however, teachers must select the lesson order they feel is appropriate and with which they feel comfortable.

- ❑ **Category of minilessons.** The first 168 minilessons, which focus on a single Building Block or Tool, are designed for use in one of four types of learning situations. These learning situations and the role of the related minilessons are 1. Introductory curricular activities: developing overall meaning for the Building Block or Tool; 2. Group practice and review activities: developing students' abilities as effective interdependent learners; 3. Independent activities: developing students' abilities as effective independent learners; and 4. Daily living skills activities: developing social skills and solving problems outside of classroom curriculum content lessons. The remaining minilessons can also accompany activities represented by one of these four categories.

- ❑ **Intent,** the specific focus of the minilesson

- ❑ **Meaning,** information about some aspect of metastrategic knowledge that can energize learning within the activity

- ❑ **Transcendence,** a bridging principle that connects the main idea of the minilesson to prior and future learning experiences in school, home, work, and social settings

Recommendations for Using Minilessons

Regardless of the content and category of the minilesson, teacher-mediators must make several decisions regarding integrating, scheduling, and modifying minilessons and building a shared metastrategic vocabulary from the minilessons. Recommendations for each type of decision follow.

Integrating Minilessons

Integrate Building Blocks of Thinking and Tools of Learning minilessons as components of a lesson on some curricular goal or school activity. They are not intended for use as self-contained lessons. Students must experience the need for each Building Block of Thinking and Tool of Learning within real learning situations. Through mediated learning experiences, students gain insight into the many aspects of each Building Block and Tool as it is applied in the classroom. While it is possible for teachers to use the minilessons related to general aspects of learning to

learn in isolation, students might not develop the insight they need to become effective learners unless the lesson connects directly to a need within some school activity in which they are engaged. Figure 4.3 presents one teacher's method for introducing Building Blocks of Thinking and Tools of Learning before minilesson integration.

FIGURE 4.3

An Introductory Lesson for Building Blocks and Tools

Bea Fisher, a CEA consultant and teacher-mediator, reports many benefits from her approach to the initial introduction of Building Blocks and Tools, including the opportunity to demonstrate an open and accepting atmosphere in the classroom and to facilitate the social construction of knowledge. The introductory lesson provides an opportunity to observe students' personal worldviews as well as their ability to communicate ideas accurately, develop a precise understanding of a concept, and analyze, synthesize, and justify information. These benefits depend on the teacher-mediator's ability to facilitate rather than lecture or tell.

When introducing any Building Block or Tool to students for the first time, Bea facilitates the development of a group mindmap in which all students analyze the Building Block or Tool by sharing and connecting their ideas about its meaning. (See the section on mindmaps in this chapter for more information about using mindmaps with CEA.) She records the shared ideas on a large sheet of paper, observing students carefully to gain a better understanding of their personal worldviews. If a student shares an incorrect or irrelevant idea, she adds this idea to the mindmap along with more helpful ideas.

After two or three more responses, Bea stops and asks the group if they see anything that does not fit well with the other ideas, explaining that something does not feel right to her. Often the person who shared the irrelevant idea recognizes the need to clarify or change it. If not, another student makes a suggestion, and Bea asks the originator of the idea to approve the change. While the class constructs the mindmap, Bea encourages students to question each other to gain a clearer understanding of what others are sharing and the connections between ideas. After exhausting the student ideas, Bea shares any important information that has not yet come up during the analysis of the Building Block or Tool.

Building a Shared Vocabulary with Minilessons

To develop a shared vocabulary of metastrategic knowledge, teacher-mediators and students must refer to the Building Blocks of Thinking and Tools of Learning as well as more general learning-to-learn concepts by their labels. Naming concepts enhances meaning and helps students think and talk about them more easily. Because these "big" words are more precise, they are often more meaningful once students understand them. Keep a dictionary in a central location in the classroom, and encourage students to announce when they need to stop and look up a new word. Have them share the definition with the class.

Some teachers of young students or students with disabilities express concerns initially that labels for some Building Blocks and Tools are too difficult for their students; however, they soon find that students are proud of the precise vocabulary they build and enjoy using it with others. Teacher-mediators should modify a label for a Building Block or Tool if they or their students derive a precise and accurate substitute that works better for their situation.

When focusing on the meaning portion of the minilesson, use language a bit above the expressive level of the students to further language development. Of course, it is important to notice when students are confused, which can occur due to lack of a connection to a school activity or lack of familiarity with the concept, rather than lack of ability to understand CEA language.

Scheduling the Use of Minilessons

Develop a schedule for the use of minilessons: determine the number of minilessons integrated into school activities each day, the number of minilessons on any one Building Block or Tool to integrate before moving on to minilessons on another Building Block or Tool, and the order of introduction of Building Blocks and Tools. Create this schedule for use of minilessons independently or with other teacher-mediators in the same setting.

Order of Minilessons

To aid memory and provide a better opportunity for relating minilessons to each other, the first 168 minilessons are grouped by the five Building Block and Tool categories. Minilessons related to the Building Blocks for approaching a learning experience appear first followed by those in the Tools for motivating behavior category as these two categories provide the most basic and general metastrategic knowledge for learning to learn. Minilessons on Building Blocks for confirming the learning experience appear next because they are important for refining the process of learning. Minilessons related to the Tools for understanding feelings and the Building Blocks for making meaning follow, respectively, because of their more abstract concepts.

Two additional groups follow these five categories. In the first set are minilessons that combine two or more Building Blocks and Tools. Students usually initiate discussions very early in CEA use about how Building Blocks and Tools relate to each other; these minilessons provide teacher-mediators with ideas on how to combine them. The final set of minilessons focuses on more general metastrategic knowledge concepts. They provide teacher-mediators with specific information students need to understand all aspects of learning to learn.

Although the minilessons are numbered, teacher-mediators will find many reasons to use the minilessons according to some other schedule. For example, some schools where all teachers use CEA have found it helpful for every teacher-mediator

to focus on the same Building Block or Tool for an entire week. Teachers inform family members and place displays throughout the school on the Building Block or Tool. The principal, librarian, and others use minilessons as well. Teacher-mediators can also select minilessons for specific situations, somewhat like selecting a recipe from a cookbook based on certain needs.

Duration and Number of Minilessons

To introduce Building Blocks and Tools, CEA consultants recommend using eight minilessons on a single Building Block or Tool before moving onto another. Also, when first introducing a given Building Block or Tool, use minilessons related to it for two to three days but no longer than one week. Students need to become familiar with the concept and its label before the integration of minilessons for other Building Blocks and Tools, but it is not necessary for students to have complete understanding before moving on.

Students need to participate in at least two, and preferably four, minilessons each day, depending on the length of time they spend with a CEA teacher-mediator. Refer to the Building Block or Tool of focus in the minilessons by name whenever it is meaningful throughout the day in all kinds of learning activities. Building Blocks and Tools are so interrelated that students learn about one through use of a minilesson on another. Teacher-mediators who have attempted to use minilessons on one Building Block or Tool until students have a complete understanding of it have found this approach counterproductive. Students become more, not less, confused with this mastery learning approach. When teacher-mediators introduce a new Building Block or Tool every few days, a spontaneous excitement occurs as students experiment with several Building Blocks and Tools, learning more about each of them as they compare similarities and differences. Even students with limited language skills do best when inquiry and messing about are valued over mastery. Mastery comes in its own time.

A small set of minilessons focus on more general aspects of learning to learn rather than specific Building Blocks of Thinking or Tools of Learning. Integrate these minilessons into school activities just like other minilessons, introducing them when most appropriate for students. Because their intents are comprehensive and encompass more information than most minilessons, use only one of the general subject minilessons on a given day. To help students make connections between these concepts and Building Blocks and Tools, use two or three minilessons on one or more Building Blocks and Tools on the same day.

After introducing all Building Blocks and Tools, teachers may use from one to four minilessons on one Building Block or Tool before moving on. Other teachers use only one minilesson, reinforcing that lesson throughout the day. Because they are always integrated into a new learning experience, teachers can use the same minilessons many times. The first year students participate in CEA classrooms, teacher-mediators should use all the minilessons at least twice. In classrooms where students remain most of the school day, teachers can integrate the mini-lessons first into basic skill subjects such as reading, written expression, and math, along with some for daily living skills. Then when using all minilessons the second time, the teachers might integrate them into subjects such as social studies and science and continue using the ones for daily living skills. After integrating all of the minilessons into learning activities at least twice, some teacher-mediators begin to develop their own minilessons.

Teachers beginning to use mediated learning teaching methods are often uncertain that students can facilitate the development of learning strategies by other students in the class. If minilessons are used consistently to help students develop metastrategic knowledge, it becomes difficult to stop young students in particular from inquiring into other people's use of Building Blocks and Tools to create learning strategies. Teacher-mediators share many stories about students as young as age 5 or 6 asking their parents, fellow students, and others about their use of Building Blocks and Tools to solve problems.

Modifying the Minilessons

The minilessons are not intended for use as lecture notes or scripts. Rather they are designed to provide ideas for teacher-mediators to use in facilitating students' thinking about Building Blocks of Thinking and Tools of Learning. Students learn more when teacher-mediators ask questions related to the intent and meaning of the minilesson rather than lecture to students. Minilessons include possible questions to help teacher-mediators establish a focus. The meaning statement also includes information that helps teacher-mediators elaborate on the information students provide and leads students to a precise understanding. The following guidelines can assist teachers with modifying minilessons.

1. Always modify the language in minilessons to match students' personal worldviews better. That is one of the important reasons not to use mini-lessons as scripts. Bridging can help everyone in the class understand each other's personal worldviews better; however, students share examples at this deep level only when the classroom is a safe and trusting environment for all (see the section on bridging in this chapter).

2. Modify minilessons according to the learning needs of students. When facilitating student participation in the minilesson, be ready to go with student ideas. The suggested questions do not have one right answer. Many ideas are acceptable as long as the student can provide a reasonable rationale. Be prepared to modify minilessons spontaneously as situations arise during a learning activity. If, for example, an unexpected learning problem develops within the learning activity, modify the minilesson to address the problem. Sometimes a different Building Block or Tool is more appropriate.

3. Build on what students already know. Help them connect a minilesson to knowledge they already possess about the learning experience and the Building Block or Tool.

4. Help students develop and use personal learning strategies that relate directly to the focus aspect of the Building Block or Tool. Do not provide expert strategies unless students need an example before they can develop their own.

5. Encourage students to compare learning strategies to see what is effective and what might improve a given strategy. Do not develop strategies that everyone should use.

6. Join with students as another learner. Share problems and the need to develop personal learning strategies based on the Building Block or Tool the lesson focuses on.

7. Allow students to connect Building Blocks and Tools they already know to the learning activity, even when planning to use a minilesson related to a specific Building Block or Tool. This practice is highly meaningful for most students and often enriches the new minilesson. In the early stages of development of the CEA teaching method, teacher-mediators were encouraged to refocus attention on the minilesson if students spontaneously interjected other Building Blocks and Tools into the minilesson. Teacher-mediators very quickly reported that this was impossible! Further, it interfered with student construction of knowledge about Building Blocks and Tools. The teacher-mediators found they could still use the minilesson they had prepared. However, students learned more by relating their knowledge about other Building Blocks and Tools.

Bridging

Through the use of minilessons, teachers integrate Building Blocks of Thinking and Tools of Learning into the regular school curriculum. Each day, teacher-mediators select several instructional activities to focus students' attention on how specific Building Blocks and Tools can help them learn more effectively in a given situation. Then teacher-mediators help students bridge the possible results of effective or ineffective use of the specific Building Block or Tool to other, personally relevant, learning experiences in and out of the school setting. Bridging, then, is a technique for connecting the use of a Building Block or Tool in one setting to its use in other settings by means of development of a general rule that applies in all settings.

Facilitating Transfer

Transfer is the ability to apply what one learns in one setting to other settings. CEA minilessons provide a method for connecting Building Blocks of Thinking and Tools of Learning to curricular activities. When teacher-mediators use minilessons regularly, students become aware of the need for specific cognitive processing behavior to learn more effectively. However, students might not transfer this knowledge readily to other situations unless teacher-mediators help them connect the need for effective use of Building Blocks and Tools to other situations.

A very important part of transfer focuses on helping students connect ways of learning at school with ways of learning at home. Families and schools have a worldview that always differs in some important ways. Students first learn to interpret the world through the patterns of thought, language, and ways of knowing of their family's culture. When they come to school, they begin to learn a new culture with or without success. It is important whatever the circumstance to transfer knowledge to and from each worldview, to accept and respect each, and to seek to understand cultural differences. Working on this transfer can help teacher-mediators develop better reciprocity with their students as they learn about the home culture while helping students make connections between home and school.

Many studies on the development of learning strategies demonstrate student difficulty in transferring strategies beyond the context and specific focus of the study (Ashman and Conway 1997). In contrast, CEA students apply learning strategies readily in a wide variety of settings in and outside school. The explanation for this success appears to be CEA's attention to conditions that research studies have shown to be necessary for transfer to occur. For example, transfer of the Tool of Self-Regulation is more likely to occur when students have talked about how they used it to build strategies in the present situation, how these strategies suggested a specific bridging principle they develop for themselves, then how this principle can help them develop personal learning strategies in other situations at school, home, work, and in social settings. Figure 4.4 presents a list of the conditions necessary for helping students prepare to transfer new learning.

Other reasons may underlie the success in student transfer that CEA teacher-mediators report. Ashman and Conway also conclude that lack of successful transfer may be due to student lack of interest in expert strategies. CEA facilitates student development of personal strategies. A further reason may well be the CEA practice of bridging originally developed by Feuerstein for use in the Instrumental Enrichment Program (Feuerstein et al. 1980).

In an example of the effects of the CEA teaching method, Juanita demonstrated an independent and effective approach to solving a personal problem. She provided her teacher with the following explanation: "Mrs. Jones, guess what? I used Exploration and Planning to make a new friend. First, I watched the girls in our class who have lots of friends. They all had their hair cut like Shannon's. So I made

FIGURE 4.4

Conditions Necessary for Transfer

Transfer takes place when

- ❏ learners see how problems resemble each other.

- ❏ learners focus on the underlying goal structure of comparable problems.

- ❏ learners are familiar with the problem domains.

- ❏ learners formulate rules to accompany examples.

- ❏ learning takes place in a social context, which fosters, generates, and contrasts justifications, principles, and explanation (Perkins and Salomin 1989).

The CEA mediated learning approach incorporates the conditions necessary for successful transfer of learning. Three basic steps of CEA bridging and the conditions of transfer they incorporate follow.

1. Connect a Building Block of Thinking or Tool of Learning to some aspect of the learning experience in which students are engaged (learners focus on underlying goal structure of problems).

2. Help students formulate a decontextualized principle that connects the Building Block of Thinking or Tool of Learning to virtually any learning experience (learners formulate rules).

3. Help students develop examples that tightly connect the decontextualized principle to examples of learning strategies in school settings, home settings, work settings, and social settings (social context fosters, generates, and contrasts justifications, principles, and explanations).

a plan to ask my mom if I could get that hair cut. She let me, but it didn't work. So I looked around our class and found that friends help each other. I made a plan to help. Yesterday, Calvin had big trouble with his math, and I asked if I could stay in at recess and help him. And now he is my friend!"

Juanita's story demonstrates her ability to carefully implement an effective approach to solving a problem. Because Juanita monitored her actions, she was able to test her plan. Indeed, Juanita reached an even higher level of active learning because she understood the need to change her approach when the first plan did not work. Juanita's strategy can be translated as a principle that applies to many other personally relevant situations: If I change my plan when it is not successful, I can solve my problem. When students connect a principle such as this to situations outside the present one, they build a framework for the transfer of Building Blocks and Tools to all kinds of learning experiences and can overcome and avoid problems that often lead to underachievement.

Integrating Bridging and Minilessons into Lessons

When integrating a CEA minilesson and bridging into a lesson activity, the discussion flows from a specific context to a decontextualized bridge back to some specific context (see Figure 4.5). First, teacher-mediators relate the cognitive processing behavior the minilesson describes to the specific lesson activity by describing its effective or ineffective use. Second, the class derives a principle that focuses on the effects of using the Building Block or Tool in any situation. Third, the class discusses examples of the principle, relating specific effects of using the Building Block or Tool in a variety of activities. This technique nurtures transfer of cognitive processing knowledge in students.

Guidelines for integrating minilessons and bridging into a lesson activity follow:

1. Introduce the lesson activity.

2. Present the minilesson near the beginning of the lesson by relating it to the given lesson activity. (Note: It is equally acceptable to present the minilesson near the end of the lesson and refer back to the lesson activity.)

3. Help students derive a principle that describes in decontextualized terms the effects of using the cognitive processing behaviors discussed in the minilesson. Make sure students use labels for the given Building Blocks and Tools in the principle and meet standards for acceptable principles described in the next section. Write the principle where all can see it.

4. Proceed with the lesson activity. (Note: If presenting the minilesson near the end of the lesson, proceed with step 5.)

5. Near the end of the lesson, refer students to the bridging principle and lead them in a discussion of at least one example from each of the four settings of school, home, work and social. Be sure the examples describe specific effects of effective or ineffective use of given Building Blocks or Tools in activities different from the lesson activity. (The first bridging example might be to tie the principle to the lesson.)

Principles in Bridging

A principle is a decontextualized rule one can apply in many situations. In bridging, the principle describes the effect of use of a given Building Block or Tool.

According to experts, for students to transfer cognitive processing behaviors, they must learn to think of their own principles rather than relying on the teacher to provide them. CEA teacher-mediators have found that even very young students can create principles successfully, especially when taught to share a principle in an "If . . . , then . . ." statement. CEA presents a structure that ensures that bridging

FIGURE 4.5

Bridging: Key Components and Sequence of Activities

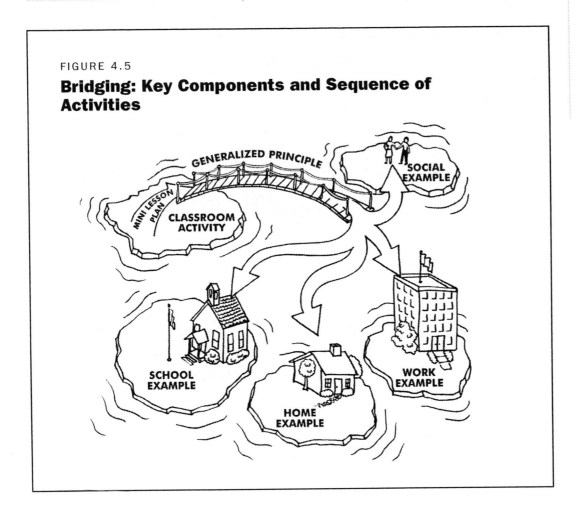

meets conditions for transfer, and teachers and students can check that justifications of examples fit principles closely. The "If . . . , then . . ." statements of decontextualized principles must contain the following characteristics:

1. The "If . . ." statement should refer by name to the Building Block or Tool and, at a more advanced level, include details about cognitive processing behavior related to the Building Block or Tool. Note: The "If . . ." statement of the principle should not mention any specific activity because it must be applicable to any learning experience. Students can then use it more readily to build learning strategies for other situations.

Acceptable beginning level "If . . ." statements

If I use Thought Integration, then . . .

If I use Precision and Accuracy, then . . .

If I use Self-Regulation and Planning, then . . .

Acceptable advanced level "If . . ." statements

If I use Planning systematically, deciding what to do first, second, third, then . . .

If I use Expression in a controlled manner, then . . .

If I think about relevant cues as I use Selective Attention, then . . .

If I make sure I use well-developed Time Concepts, then . . .

Unacceptable "If . . ." statements

If I use Selective Attention to find my pencil, then . . . (Unacceptable "If . . ." statement because it mentions a specific activity.)

If I use Precision and Accuracy when I listen to the teacher's instructions, then . . . (Unacceptable "If . . ." statement because it mentions an activity related to the school setting only.)

If I know my right from my left, then . . . (Unacceptable "If . . ." statement because it does not use a Building Block or Tool label.)

2. The "then . . ." statement should refer to a result or an effect of using the Building Block or Tool (and, at the advanced level, the cognitive processing behavior) that applies to many activities from school, home, work, and social settings. Note: The "then . . ." statement of the principle should not mention a specific activity because it is a decontextualized principle that must apply to any situation.

Acceptable principles

If I use Thought Integration effectively, then I will be able to combine all the pieces of information I need.

If I use Self-Regulation and Planning, then learning becomes easier.

If I use Planning systematically, deciding what to do first, second, and third, then I can solve problems.

If I use Expression in a controlled manner, then I make fewer mistakes.

If I think about relevant cues as I use Selective Attention, then I can concentrate on specific learning needs.

If I use well-developed Time Concepts, then I avoid problems.

Unacceptable principles

If I use Expression in a controlled manner, then I will get along better with others. (Unacceptable principle as "then . . ." statement mentions a resulting behavior that is limited to a social interaction and cannot be applied to

school, home, and work activities other than social interactions in those settings.)

If I use Planning systematically, deciding what to do first, second, and third, then I will be able to do my arithmetic homework. (Unacceptable principle as "then . . ." statement mentions a specific activity.)

If I think about relevant cues as I use Selective Attention, then I will be able to write the letters of the alphabet. (Unacceptable principle as "then . . ." statement mentions a specific activity.)

Using Examples in Bridging

Examples show how the principle applies to activities in virtually any situation. When bridging, it is important that students discuss examples from several settings so they understand that Building Blocks and Tools are not just for school learning. To ensure transfer, always request examples from each of the following four situations: 1. school, including all types of learning activities other than the current one; 2. home, including all types of work and leisure activities related to family life; 3. work, including all types of activities related to vocational skills; and 4. social, including all types of interpersonal relationships in school, home, and work settings.

Examples facilitate transfer much more effectively if they relate closely to the bridging principle. Examples should describe learning strategies based on the cause and effect stated in the principle. Students are most successful in providing examples if teacher-mediators and other students encourage them to justify the connection between each aspect of the bridging principle and their learning strategy in the example they supply. For example, students agree to use the following bridging principle: "If I use Exploration to gather information systematically, then I will be able to solve my problems." Then one student shares an example that is partially but not adequately matched to the principle: "At home I use Exploration to look for my toys." This example does not describe how the student used Exploration to gather information systematically or what problem was solved. The teacher or other students need to ask the student to describe the problem and to explain how gathering information systematically helped. The student might then say, "Well, my problem was that I couldn't find my toy cars, so I asked Mom, then my brother, and then my sister if they had seen them. My brother had thrown them in my closet after he tripped on one."

Some teacher-mediators and students prefer to state examples in the same "If . . . , then . . ." format as the principle. Others find this too structured and awkward.

Acceptable bridging examples

The following are examples to accompany a principle derived from a discussion of the need for Thought Integration in the activity of counting: If I use Thought Integration, then I will be able to combine all the pieces of information I need.

School: If I use Thought Integration when I practice my handwriting, then I will be able to remember to put a bigger space between words than between letters.

Home: If I use Thought Integration when putting away my toys at home, then I will be able to control my thinking about where each toy goes.

Work: If I use Thought Integration when mowing the grass, then I will be able to control my thinking so I follow all the safety rules.

Social: If I use Thought Integration when dealing with my mom, then I will be able to control my thinking as I try to convince her to let me spend the night with my best friend.

Unacceptable bridging examples

School: If I use Thought Integration, then I will be able to count my pencils that I use at school. (Unacceptable as the example is the same as the lesson activity.)

Home: If I use Thought Integration, then I will be able to control my thinking as I put away my toys. (Unacceptable as "If . . ." statement does not mention home.)

Work: If I control my thinking, then I will be able to mow the grass. (Unacceptable as the example does not include the label for the Building Block.)

Social: If I use Thought Integration, then I will try to convince Mom to let me spend the night with my best friend. (Unacceptable as the example does not clearly relate Thought Integration to the task of convincing Mom.)

Use of Bridging with Minilessons

Teachers use minilessons to help students transfer metastrategic knowledge by means of bridging examples students provide. In their bridging examples, students develop learning strategies based on a bridging principle related to a Building Block or Tool for use in other home, school, work, and social settings. The following are guidelines for using bridging techniques with minilessons.

1. Always use the bridging technique with each minilesson. Do not bridge until after students have insight into the minilesson as it relates to the learning activity and lesson in which it is integrated. When students have insight, they can talk easily about how the Building Block or Tool fits within the lesson according to the focus of the minilesson. Do bridging at the end of the activity, even when introducing the minilesson much earlier in the activity. Use student-developed bridging principles rather than those

provided in the transcendence part of the minilesson, which are examples to stimulate thinking.

2. If students have difficulty, provide the "If . . ." part of the bridging principle, and ask them to provide the "then . . ." part.

3. Make certain bridging examples fit the chosen principle precisely. Elicit one example for each of the four settings: home, school, work, and social.

4. Help students develop their own bridging principles in a variety of ways. Successful approaches include the following:

   • Ask students for several suggestions, writing them on the board for everyone to see. Have students decide if they meet the standards for bridging principles: they have a label for a Building Block or Tool, and they are decontextualized so they apply in any home, school, work, or social situation. Finally, have students select one bridging principle from the acceptable choices based on the following criteria: 1. principle meets rules for being acceptable; 2. the principle fits the minilesson; and 3. students think the principle is a good one.

   • Inform students during the minilesson that the class will stop and bridge whenever someone thinks of a bridging principle.

   • Have students write bridging principles and examples as part of journal writing. This approach is appropriate only when students have learned to write acceptable bridging principles and examples that fit the principles precisely.

Developing New Minilessons

As teacher-mediators become more expert in using CEA, their desire to adapt and develop minilessons that meet the needs of specific students increases. The more meaningful minilessons are for students, the greater their ability to help students gain important insight into knowledge essential to becoming an effective, independent and interdependent learner. Personalized minilessons are always more meaningful, as long as they result in high quality mediated learning experiences. For more information on why and how to provide high quality mediated learning experiences, see Chapter 2. For tools to help in reflecting on a teacher-mediator's role and ways of interacting, see Chapter 5.

To adapt and develop effective minilessons, teachers analyze the thinking process that underlies the development of a minilesson. Each of the three sections of a minilesson plays an important role in the thinking process. However, the development of a minilesson actually begins with teachers thinking about the learning activity in which they plan to integrate it.

A minilesson must fit a school activity whether the activity focuses on academic learning or a daily living skill such as getting along with others. To make a tight fit, teacher-mediators must analyze the activity to determine any anticipated learning problems for which a Building Block or Tool would help and the intent of the activity. The learning problems might relate directly to academic skills needed to engage in the activity or to problems students may have in working with others, organizing ideas, or some other requirement of the task itself or the intent of the activity as it relates to learning to learn. Teacher-mediators should think about intent in relation to its benefit to students beyond the task. This analysis should focus on how the activity contributes to major goals for students such as meeting specific academic standards, engaging successfully in more advanced learning related to the subject matter, and adapting and contributing to society as adults. After this thinking, teacher-mediators select a particular Building Block or Tool based on how well it can help students overcome the problem or meet the intent of the activity.

After analyzing the curricular or other school activity and selecting a Building Block or Tool, teacher-mediators analyze and synthesize the three parts of a minilesson: intent, meaning, and transcendence. The intent statement is actually an objective for the ideas that teacher-mediators want to communicate about a Building Block or Tool or learning to learn in general. It should closely match the bridging principle found in the transcendence statement. While developing a minilesson, teacher-mediators go back and forth developing tentative statements for the intent and transcendence sections until they connect to each other and to the school activity. Next, they develop the meaning section of the minilesson and make final changes in the intent and transcendence statement.

The meaning section of the minilesson should focus on how to facilitate students' reflection on one or more aspects of a given Building Block or Tool, which involves creating a need for the information. Students are much more likely to retain and use the information from the minilesson if they have a clear need to understand it. Teacher-mediators plan how to help students recognize a need within the activity for the minilesson information, then they consider specific questions that can help students derive the information for themselves.

Sometimes it is necessary to share new information related to Building Blocks and Tools by lecturing briefly. Much more often, however, students have the knowledge within them and need only help from teacher-mediators in making it explicit and applying it to specific needs within an activity. Learning is greatly enhanced when students realize that they do possess knowledge about how to learn. Whenever possible, teacher-mediators should ask rather than tell. Once they develop a plan for facilitating learning in this way, teacher-mediators need to double-check that the ideas in the meaning section accomplish the intent of the

minilesson and lead to student development of principles similar to the transcendence statement.

Adapting Minilessons for Specific Settings

Teacher-mediators can adapt CEA minilessons for use in a wide variety of settings from kindergarten through adult basic education classes. This section provides suggestions for adapting the minilessons in specific settings. It is important to couple these suggestions with a basic premise underlying CEA: all teaching should consider each student's personal worldview and culture. Teacher-mediators strive for reciprocity with each student as they engage with them in mediated learning experiences.

No matter what the educational setting or learner age, use the following guidelines for minilessons. Additional tips for use with specific learners follow these general guidelines.

Use the labels. Expect students of all ages to learn and use the labels for Building Blocks of Thinking and Tools for Learning. They will not be nearly as successful in using metastrategic knowledge and learning how to learn unless they have a label for each Building Block and Tool.

Display icons. Place icons with the labels for each Building Block of Thinking and Tool for Learning in the classroom where students can see them. Provide students with their own booklets of the icons, labels, and definitions so family members can help them use the concepts accurately (see Appendix).

Modify minilessons for group size. Adapt the minilessons designed for independent and small-group activities for large-group activities or pairs of students.

Modify minilesson language. Put minilesson information into language appropriate for students. Children develop ability with language most effectively when adults talk to them using language that is more advanced than theirs. It is necessary, however, to connect this advanced language with something the child knows and can perceive.

Use concrete examples. For any age learner, it is very helpful to connect abstract thoughts to concrete examples. Teacher-mediators can best accomplish this by integrating minilessons into activities that actively engage students. It is also important to create a need for using the Building Block and Tool within the activity. Remember, the intent of each minilesson applies just as well to nonacademic learning activities as to academic subject matter.

Use bridging. Always include bridging with the minilessons. With learners of all ages, provide models and assistance in developing bridging principles and examples. Display bridging principles in writing.

Limit focus time. Use minilessons for a given Building Block or Tool for two days to one week. Help students refer to that Building Block or Tool throughout the school day. After no more than one week, focus on another Building Block or Tool.

Allow students to talk about other Building Blocks and Tools within a minilesson and at other times as appropriate, making sure they connect them accurately to the current learning experience.

Adapting Minilessons for Kindergarten and Students Not Yet Reading

Use the labels. Young children, especially, are proud of their ability to talk about Building Blocks and Tools and their mastery of the labels.

Modify minilessons for group size. When modifying minilessons, note that young students often work better in pairs than in a group of three or four students. They also need more focus on social skills than older students do.

Use concrete examples. The need to use concrete examples when discussing abstract concepts such as Working Memory or Inner Meaning is even more important with young students.

Use bridging. Because kindergarten students are most likely unable to read bridging principles and examples displayed, read them aloud. Keep them brief to make them easier to remember. Point out how examples fit each part of the principle.

Adapting Minilessons for Special Education Students with Lower Cognitive Functioning

Use the labels. Expect students to learn and use the labels or, if nonverbal, to learn to recognize others' use of them. Although these students may need more time to become fluent with the labels, their use of the labels enhances their ability to learn how to learn.

Modify minilessons for group size. Some special education students work better with a partner than on a larger team. They usually benefit from being a part of mixed ability groups; however, other students need to learn how not to co-opt their learning. The use of Building Blocks and Tools to help in learning social skills can greatly improve the participation of special needs students in collaborative and cooperative learning activities.

Use concrete examples. Connecting abstract thoughts to concrete examples is especially important with special education students. It is also important to be very careful to create a need for using the Building Block and Tool within the activity and to help students connect concrete thinking to more abstract thinking.

Use bridging. Even with students who cannot read, display bridging principles in writing. Expect students to develop examples that connect accurately to the principle. Point out how examples fit each part of the principle. Encourage students to share examples that help others understand their personal worldview. Build an open and trusting atmosphere within the classroom so students are more willing to talk about challenges that are significant enough for them to be placed in special education.

Limit focus time. Use minilessons for a given Building Block or Tool for two days to one week. After no more than one week, focus on another Building Block or Tool. Understanding of one Building Block or Tool can help students learn others, and each student finds special meaning in different Building Blocks or Tools. Do not insist on mastery before introducing more concepts.

Adapting Minilessons for Students with English as a Second Language

Use the labels. Use the labels for Building Blocks of Thinking and Tools for Learning in the student's native language before having students learn them in English.

Display icons. Display icons with the labels for each Building Block of Thinking and Tool for Learning in English and, if possible, in students' native language.

Use concrete examples. Connect minilesson ideas to something students know and can perceive. Refer to pictures and objects. Check to make sure students understand discussions in English. Use students' native language when possible.

Use bridging. Encourage students to develop bridging examples that focus on learning a second language or overcoming problems of not knowing a language very well. As with any students, provide models and assistance in developing bridging principles and examples. Use bridging to build an understanding of pride in one's own culture and respect for the culture of others. Develop an open and trusting environment where students are comfortable in sharing information with each other about their culture and different ways of doing. Focus also on examples that highlight the hidden expectations in school for knowing how, where, and when to do something according to a worldview held by the school that may differ from the worldview of those from a different culture. Display bridging principles in writing, and point to words while reading them aloud.

Adapting Minilessons for Use with Adult Learners

Modify minilessons for group size. Some adult learners prefer to work alone or with a partner rather than on a larger team. They usually benefit most, however, from being a part of mixed ability groups. As with any learners, it is important they learn not to co-opt other students' learning. Social skills may need attention even by the most advanced students.

Use concrete examples. As with any learners, build on students' past experiences and what they already know and understand. Help these students value their abilities by talking with them about how they use their knowledge and experience to help their families and community.

Use bridging. Encourage students to share examples that help others understand their personal worldviews. Build an open and trusting atmosphere within the classroom so students are more willing to talk about their challenges in learning.

Limit focus time. Use minilessons for a given Building Block or Tool long enough to ensure familiarity. Help students refer to the Building Block or Tool throughout their time in class. Introduce other Building Blocks or Tools as soon as students can use the focus one at some basic level. Understanding of one Building Block or Tool can help students learn others. Each student finds special meaning in different Building Blocks or Tools. Do not insist on mastery before introducing more concepts.

Adapting Minilessons for Use in a Culturally Diverse Setting

Use bridging. Develop bridging into a major part of the minilesson. Highlight personal worldviews and family practices in bridging examples. Show students how important these practices are in learning to learn. Show students how much everyone benefits by learning about others' ways of doing things.

Show caring and respect for every student and insist that other students exhibit respect for others. Strive to establish an open, trusting, and safe atmosphere where all students feel welcome to share their personal worldviews and culture, and class members have pride in their own culture and respect for the culture of others. Join with students in sharing cultural and family activities. Demonstrate an appropriate way to share beliefs and personal worldviews that does not assume that others must agree with these beliefs and views to be accepted.

Adapting Minilessons for Small-Group or One-on-One Learning

Display icons. Display icons and refer to labels for Building Blocks and Tools just as with a larger group of students. Give students copies of icons and definitions so they can use them in other classes and at home. Share the copies with other teachers and with parents so they can help students use Building Blocks and Tools in learning experiences in which they participate. Keep other teachers and parents informed about which Building Block or Tool the student is learning to use.

Modify minilessons for group size. Because small-group or one-on-one learning allows teacher-mediators to focus more on individual students than is possible in larger groups, teachers can select and adapt minilessons for Building Blocks and Tools based on students' specific needs. They can also introduce new Building Blocks and Tools based on each student's interests and needs.

If the teacher-mediator working with a small group or one-on-one is the only CEA teacher with whom the student spends time, the teacher needs to mediate and use minilessons for all Building Blocks and Tools. Students can help decide which one to learn next. If the student is in classes with other CEA teacher-mediators using minilessons with a large group of students, then this teacher-mediator should reinforce the use of Building Blocks and Tools of focus in the large-group setting. At the same time, this teacher-mediator can also use other minilessons that focus on Building Blocks or Tools selected by the student or the teacher.

The small-group or one-on-one teacher-mediator can share much valuable information with other teachers and family members about Building Blocks and Tools a student needs most.

Modify minilesson language. The minilessons are written in words intended to communicate clearly information to the teacher-mediator. Teacher-mediators always need to express them in language that is responsive to their students' personal worldviews and culture.

Use bridging. Both the teacher and students should provide bridging examples, especially if working one-on-one. It is important to think about examples that apply to more than one person. The teacher-mediator should work especially hard at joining with the student as another learner in this type of setting. It is important to see how other learners use strategies within the same learning experience.

Adapting Minilessons for Classes such as Art, Music, Physical Education, and the Library

Communicate with colleagues. Work with other teacher-mediators to establish a system for knowing the focus Building Block or Tool in other classes. Help students transfer what they are learning in other classes to this nonacademic class. Allow students to connect other Building Blocks and Tools to the lesson as long as they can explain their relevance.

In nonacademic classes, it is often possible to help students develop very clear insight into Building Blocks and Tools perhaps because of the more concrete nature of activities in such classes. Therefore, it is very important to include teachers in these classes as important CEA users in the school. Teachers of nonacademic subjects can provide important information to other teachers. Because they work with students from many different classes, they can readily compare students' general ability in using Building Blocks and Tools. They can provide teachers with information about students' abilities to transfer knowledge about Building Blocks and Tools to nonacademic activities. In addition, they can identify teachers who are especially successful in helping students learn Building Blocks and Tools so they can share their successful techniques with other teacher-mediators.

Use minilessons. Integrate minilessons into class activities just as teacher-mediators do in academic classes. Include bridging, spending more time on examples that relate to the focus of this class as they affect home, school, work, and social settings.

Because teachers of nonacademic subjects do not usually work with students as frequently as other teachers do, they need to adapt the frequency of introducing new Building Blocks and Tools. If students have other CEA classes, this teacher can select one minilesson per class period on the same Building Block or Tool that other teachers have selected for focus. If students are learning about Building Blocks and Tools only in this nonacademic class, then the teacher needs to introduce a new Building Block or Tool each week while using a minilesson in every class session. It is also important to schedule review weeks during which the class uses more minilessons for a Building Block or Tool introduced a few weeks earlier. The particular schedule depends on students' needs. A review week might take place every second or third week for the first few Building Blocks and Tools and less often as students learn these concepts more easily.

Mindmapping

Another CEA practice involves the use of mindmapping, a type of graphic organizer. Mindmapping allows students to see connections between a concept of the lesson and other concepts outside the lesson. It helps students transfer subject matter knowledge. Mindmapping has several purposes. The technique

- ❑ helps students transfer subject matter knowledge,
- ❑ helps students connect school learning to the real world,
- ❑ promotes students' awareness of the need to make connections among concepts at several levels,
- ❑ provides opportunities to focus on different worldviews by recording thoughts from many students in the classroom, and
- ❑ provides a visual aid for students in organizing and categorizing information.

Teacher-mediators can develop a mindmap as part of the lesson plan and display it during the lesson. Or the class might create a mindmap spontaneously during the lesson. In this second case, teacher-mediators watch for situations during the lesson where mindmapping would be helpful such as when students are describing various aspects of a concept or topic, trying to get the main idea of a concept or topic, or exploring what they already know about a concept or topic before beginning a lesson or project.

Each mindmap should meet the following criteria:

- ❑ A mindmap contains a minimum of five concepts.
- ❑ A mindmap connects a broader concept to several secondary level concepts.
- ❑ A mindmap includes one or more tertiary levels of concepts.
- ❑ A mindmap connects a subject matter concept to other concepts outside the lesson. (The subject matter concept may appear at any level on the map.)

One of the purposes of mindmapping is to help students relate a new idea to its place within a larger framework; therefore, it is important to connect a broader, more encompassing concept to several aspects of it, ie., superordinate to subordinates. For example, the word or phrase in the center bubble of a mindmap repre-

sents the superordinate concept; for example, *trees*. The bubbles directly connected to the center one are the ordinate concepts such as *evergreen* and *deciduous*. The bubbles connected to one of the ordinate concepts are subordinate concepts such as *pine* and *fir* connected to the *evergreen* ordinate bubble. The idea taken from the current learning situation may be the broader concept itself or one of several aspects of the broader concept. The goal is to help students get the big picture (see sample mindmap, Figure 4.6).

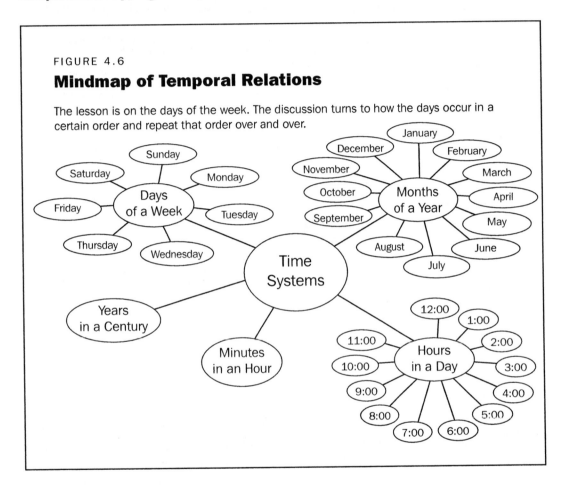

FIGURE 4.6

Mindmap of Temporal Relations

The lesson is on the days of the week. The discussion turns to how the days occur in a certain order and repeat that order over and over.

Lesson Planning Guide

Teachers can best meet the needs of students when they create activities that allow students to learn at an individually meaningful and appropriate level in a safely challenging, interactive, and discovery-oriented way. Teachers cannot personalize learning for students as much as is beneficial unless they provide activities that encourage students to make choices and take responsibility for choosing what is meaningful. Through high quality mediated learning, teachers seek continuously to work with students in their zones of proximal development, in that small window of learning opportunity where students are challenged but not frustrated. During the beginning stages of learning how to integrate metastrategic knowledge and bridging as components of school activities, the lesson planning guide (see Figure 4.7) helps teacher-mediators think about essential aspects of lessons. Using this guide, teacher-mediators find that they can compare subject matter objectives with minilesson objectives and gain a deeper insight into the purpose of learning. This insight leads to collaboration with other teachers in the school and helps everyone better understand the scope and sequence of their curriculum and, especially, the purpose of their curricular focus.

Implementation of the lesson plan is flexible. While it is very important for teacher-mediators to focus on the development of metastrategic knowledge within the lesson through the use of the minilesson, they can and should adapt the plan for the lesson as needed. For example, teacher-mediators cannot know for certain whether the lesson plan will put students into their zones of proximal development. They might need to adapt parts of the lesson so it is more challenging or less frustrating or even more personally relevant to students.

Facilitating Interdependent Learning

One of the most powerful practices for facilitating mediated learning in the classroom is the use of collaborative and cooperative learning. In CEA, mediated learning builds on the development of independent learning skills as they interact with the development of interdependent learning skills.

Collaborative learning is learning that takes place among two or more people, where ideas develop that belong to the group rather than any one individual. Collaborative learning focuses on inquiry over advocacy of ideas and suspending assumptions so the group members can explore the ideas of all members. Cooperative learning is a set of techniques for group learning that may or may not be collaborative. It is based on four principles: positive interdependence, individual accountability, equal participation, and simultaneous interaction.

Many teachers use cooperative learning in the classroom to facilitate the development of interdependent learning skills, to make learning more enjoyable, and to provide more active learning time for all students. Some teachers, however, are reluctant to integrate cooperative learning into their classes because of problems they have observed with its use in the past. CEA experience demonstrates that teachers can overcome these problems in a relatively short time when the classroom is a laboratory for learning in which students act as mediators for each other and develop learning strategies for themselves and their group based on Building Blocks and Tools.

A consultant with a high level of expertise in the use of cooperative learning worked with CEA teacher-mediators weekly for one year. She noted a synergistic

FIGURE 4.7

Lesson Planning Guide

The lesson planning guide is designed to help teacher-mediators integrate minilessons and bridging into subject matter lessons by describing the main parts of any lesson within the context of the lesson.

1. **Description of Curriculum Content**

   What is the specific subject matter focus?

2. **Lesson Objectives**

   What is (are) the lesson objective(s) related directly to the subject matter? What is (are) the lesson objective(s) related directly to a Building Block of Thinking, Tool of Learning, or more general aspect of learning to learn? (Note: This objective can be the Intent statement in a minilesson.)

3. **Sequence of Lesson Activities**

   What activities will take place within the lesson? What is the most likely sequence of events? Which minilesson will be used? Where will it fit into the lesson? (Note: List the steps of the lesson. Be as detailed or general as is helpful.)

4. **Bridging Principle**

   What decontextualized principle ("If . . . , then . . ." statement) could one draw out of the minilesson as integrated with the subject matter? (Note: Use this principle only if students are unable to develop their own. Be sure the principle meets the critical attributes of CEA bridging principles.)

5. **Bridging Examples**

   Prepare examples of the bridging principle to share with students as they use the principle to build learning strategies for use in home, school, work, and social situations. (Note: Share these to join students as another learner and to provide needed examples if students cannot provide examples. Be sure all examples meet the critical attributes for bridging examples in CEA.)

effect taking place in CEA classrooms. Students in CEA classes were much more effective at developing skills while engaged in highly challenging, inquiry-learning, collaborative and cooperative learning activities. In fact, teams of students were successful—and expressed a joy in learning—as they used high quality educational software normally introduced two or more grade levels above their level.

To facilitate the development of interdependent learning skills, teachers should understand the sources of problems in the use of cooperative learning and solutions for overcoming the problems provided by the CEA comprehensive teaching method. A description of these sources and solutions appears in Figure 4.8.

For students to develop the interdependent learning skills that can help them become effective facilitators of mediated learning, they must understand attitudes that govern the way they relate to others as a member of a community engaged in collaborative and cooperative learning. When class members have positive atti-

---

FIGURE 4.8

Difficulties with Cooperative Learning

The following are common sources of difficulty in the use of cooperative learning in the classroom and CEA solutions for overcoming them.

Source: Inadequate interdependent learning skills

Solutions:

❏ Build awareness of positive attitudes of effective team members.

❏ Conduct frequent self-evaluation and team evaluation of needed social skills.

❏ Learn to use questions that lead to inquiry rather than advocacy (Would you say more about _____? Why did you ask that question?).

❏ Conduct self-evaluation and team evaluation of the occurrence of collaborative learning.

Source: Inadequate independent learning skills

Solutions:

❏ Facilitate mediated learning experiences by teacher and students.

❏ Use Building Blocks and Tools to develop personal and team learning strategies.

Source: Lack of awareness and use of cooperative learning skills such as positive interdependence, individual accountability, equal opportunity, and simultaneous learning

Solution:

❏ Use mediated learning to develop insight into the importance of the principles.

❏ Select activities for which students need to be mindful of principles.

❏ Assign or have team members select roles that monitor team use of principles (gatekeeper who ensures all participate equally, reflector who focuses attention on individual accountability).

---

tudes, they learn social skills more easily. Hargrove (1995, 1998) describes attitudes of team members engaged in collaborative work. Figure 4.9 presents an adaptation of these attitudes for use in CEA classrooms.

It is important to note that not all cooperative learning incorporates collaborative learning. Certainly, most cooperative learning methods do not rely on a mediated learning approach nor do they use a shared vocabulary for metastrategic knowledge. Teacher-mediators who combine all three enhance the synergistic effect. As a result, students learn the skills needed to function collaboratively in a much more effective manner. They are also able to solve individual and group problems by drawing on their metastrategic knowledge to build learning strategies.

FIGURE 4.9

Positive Attitudes of Interdependent Members of a Laboratory for Learning

❏ I am related to other members of our class and want to build a shared vision.

❏ I am committed to our laboratory for learning and try to inspire my classmates.

❏ I balance advocacy of my ideas with inquiry into my own and my classmates' views.

❏ I learn from mistakes and try to see how I contribute to my own problems.

❏ I work hard to be a part of our learning community and know that this is the way to really look good.

A class cannot adequately use the combination of collaborative and cooperative learning, mediated learning, and a shared vocabulary for metastrategic knowledge unless learning activities exhibit characteristics appropriate for use in a laboratory for learning. CEA provides a means for evaluating activities (see the critical attributes for activities in a laboratory for learning in Figure 2.8).

Team Effort and Support in CEA Use

Some teacher-mediators find it simple to integrate minilessons and bridging as components of curricular and daily living skills activities. A higher percentage of teacher-mediators feel considerably challenged during the first few weeks of using minilessons and bridging. Experienced teacher-mediators have demonstrated the importance of several factors in determining success in using CEA to help students become effective, independent, interdependent, and lifelong learners.

First, teacher-mediators must make a firm commitment to use the minilessons, beginning the day they return to the classroom after attending a CEA workshop. Insight into the Building Blocks and Tools—and learning to learn in general—builds as teacher-mediators and students think about them in real situations and use them to build learning strategies.

Teacher-mediators do not develop expertise by merely reading this handbook. They have to experience CEA to learn it. This sometimes challenging way for teachers to learn something they must teach can be highly successful when teacher-mediators join students as another learner and share their own anxieties about learning. This technique is a powerful way to mediate to students.

One excellent CEA teacher-mediator shared a story every day with his students about some personal experience in which a learning strategy constructed from a specific Building Block or Tool could have helped or did help him overcome a problem at home, at school, or in the community. His students, even those with behavior problems, were eager to hear his stories. Far from thinking less of their teacher, they admired his courage and learned an exceedingly important lesson for life: everyone has learning problems, and everyone can find ways to face them and work to overcome them.

Many teacher-mediators have found it helpful to set group goals for using the minilessons. Teacher-mediators working at the same level, or sometimes all the teacher-mediators in a school, agree to use two to four minilessons per day. In some cases they work together to plan curriculum lessons based on the same minilessons. Some schools decide that all classes will focus on the same Building Block or Tool for an entire week. They agree to use the eight minilessons related to the Building Block or Tool one or more times during the week. Often these schools send home a one-page explanation of the Building Block or Tool that also encourages family members to talk about the need for the concept throughout the week and to place the page where all family members see it.

Teacher-mediators often find it helpful to ask students to share the personal meaning they find in the Building Blocks and Tools. One first-grade teacher-mediator asked her students to pick out the Building Block or Tool they found most meaningful and write down their reasons for their choices. She was amazed to discover that every student had selected the Building Block or Tool that they most needed to build strategies for using. For example, one very impulsive child selected Exploration. A student who needed to engage in more purposeful behavior selected Goal Orientation. These results encouraged the teacher to set goals that helped her go further in turning her classroom into a laboratory for learning.

Some of the best CEA teacher-mediators say it takes about two years to become comfortable with all aspects of CEA. It is important, then, for teacher-mediators to be patient with their learning. Quick fixes are easily learned but do not help students maximize their learning potential.

CEA Best Teaching Practices

The following list of thirteen best teaching practices for CEA lessons summarizes for teacher-mediators the components of an effective lesson in which CEA practices have been fully implemented.

1. **Focus students' attention on specific objectives and guide the lesson in a chosen direction.** Determine objectives for every lesson, and redirect the discussion when necessary back toward the objectives of the lesson. Demonstrate the quality of intent.

2. **Respond to students' behavior in a timely and appropriate manner.** Watch for new insight just gained by a student and provide feedback. Attempt to include or acknowledge every student. React to off-task behavior in a manner that gets students back on task. Employ reciprocity.

3. **Clearly express an emotional attachment and involvement with students.** Demonstrate caring and concern for students' feelings. Share personal reactions to situations. Help students feel connected to you as a fellow human being. Demonstrate the quality of meaning.

4. **Discuss how the subject matter relates to prior and future learning experiences.** Connect the subject matter to its use outside of school in the real world as well as to other school tasks. Go beyond any specific context. Engage in transcendence.

5. **Connect the subject matter to related knowledge within its domain framework.** Show students how this concept relates to its subparts as well as other concepts at the same level and how all these relate to a relevant but broader concept. For example, when teaching short-vowel sounds, show the connection between specific short-vowel sounds, then relate this lesson to long-vowel sounds at the same level, then the entire discussion to sounding out words or to reading. Engage in transcendence.

6. **Encourage students to use Self-Regulation and to find an effective personal approach to the learning experience.** Draw plans and strategies for working from students whenever possible. Share a personal strategy only when they cannot come up with something effective. Always ask before telling.

7. **Involve all students in discussions.** Ask questions in a manner that encourages everyone to think of a response, inquire into what others are saying, and learn collaboratively.

8. **Use mediated learning when students need assistance, and encourage students to help mediate learning experiences with each other.** Do not co-opt. Give students time to rethink their inadequate responses, develop personal learning strategies to help solve the problem, and demonstrate their improved understanding in some way.

9. **Ask students to think about their performance and self-evaluate.** Have students state the adequacy of their responses and their reasons for saying so.

10. **Select or have students select one or more Building Blocks or Tools and discuss how its use affects performance in the given situation.** Integrate a minilesson into the learning activity. Always work for student insight from the lesson.

11. **Bridge the selected Building Block or Tool from a principle the students develop.** Adapt the transcendence statement from the minilesson if necessary. Make sure the principle is a decontextualized rule and is an "If . . ., then . . ." statement. Help students connect their bridging examples for home, school, work, and social situations very tightly with the cause and effect statement of the principle.

12. **Use mindmapping to help students get the big picture about school learning and transfer school learning to the real world.** Cluster appropriate concepts together. Encourage spontaneity in building mindmaps.

13. **Model Building Blocks and Tools by sharing personal examples of effective or ineffective use.** Relate the use of one or more in planning and presenting the lesson on how lack of effective use caused difficulty.

Chapter 5

REFLECTING ON COGNITIVE ENRICHMENT ADVANTAGE USE

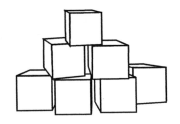

The Need for Self-Reflection

The value of teacher self-reflection became apparent early in Cognitive Enrichment Advantage (CEA) workshops. While workshops always included opportunities for reflection and discussion, workshop leaders controlled the reflection through specially designed learning activities based on concept analysis theory. Participants also engaged in challenging, problem-solving simulations that allowed them to gain insight into their own cognitive processes and affective-motivational approaches to learning that they would later mediate to their students. But eventually the structured approach of the reflection practices gave way to the needs of workshop participants. Letting them reflect on personal insights into their own classrooms and students proved the most valuable workshop lesson of all. Current CEA workshops provide activities that help teachers reflect on their own teaching practices.

This reflection must continue beyond the workshops. Teachers must establish personal goals to move toward their vision as a teacher-mediator who maximizes learning potential. When reflecting on these goals, teachers should do the following:

❑ Make time to record reflections in a journal on a regular basis, at least weekly.

❑ Participate in support meetings weekly or as often as possible.

❑ Work with a teaching partner and provide each other with feedback.

❑ Make several videotapes of the classroom, and when reviewing them, focus on mediation skills.

❑ Review the elements of highly effective mediated learning experiences (Figure 5.1).

❑ Complete the Checklist of CEA Teacher-Mediator Qualities in this chapter, one segment at a time, to reflect on teacher behaviors that enhance mediated learning.

❑ Reflect on personal and student use of the Building Blocks and Tools with the self-reflection prompts found in this chapter.

❑ Participate in dialogues on the CEA website.

❑ Attend CEA workshops on facilitating change and share successes and challenges.

FIGURE 5.1

Striving for Excellence: Elements of Highly Effective Mediated Learning Experiences

Teacher-mediators must reflect on the components of effective mediated learning experiences. Initially, teacher-mediators model these elements. Over time, students can learn to accept joint responsibility for their occurrence. Teacher-mediators need to strive for inclusion of at least one aspect from each of the five elements as often as possible.

1. Nurturing Learners
   - ❏ Maintain an open classroom atmosphere.
   - ❏ Avoid co-opting.
   - ❏ Seek reciprocity.
   - ❏ Focus on Tools of Learning for understanding feelings and striving to motivate oneself.
   - ❏ Include individual, small-group, and large-group learning experiences.

2. Questioning the Learning Process
   - ❏ Ask questions that encourage reflection among all members of the classroom community (ask rather than tell).
   - ❏ Explore various Building Blocks of Thinking and Tools of Learning that are relevant to the learning experience.
   - ❏ Evaluate the degree of effectiveness of independent learning through focus on Building Blocks of Thinking and Tools of Learning (self-evaluation and constructive feedback from others).
   - ❏ Evaluate the degree of effectiveness of interdependent learning through focus on Building Blocks of Thinking, Tools of Learning, and social skill focus (self-evaluation and team evaluation).
   - ❏ Order events in the learning process and predict outcomes of learning.

3. Developing Personal Learning Strategies
   - ❏ Help students construct personal strategies based on knowledge about one or more Building Blocks of Thinking and Tools of Learning.
   - ❏ Explore various adaptations of learning strategies and reasons for adaptations.
   - ❏ Compare the effectiveness of various learning strategies.

4. Challenging and Seeking Justification
   - ❏ Create positive stress within the learning experience to help students move into zones of proximal development.
   - ❏ Confirm the effectiveness of students' thinking through reflection on Building Blocks, and confirm their feelings and motivation through reflection on Tools of Learning.
   - ❏ Encourage students to strive for excellence by seeking high goals.

5. Seeking Relationships
   - ❏ Connect school learning to prior and future real-world experiences.
   - ❏ Connect prior knowledge to what students want to learn.
   - ❏ Use systemic thinking to connect concepts to broader and smaller concepts.
   - ❏ Analyze and synthesize concepts within and across domains.
   - ❏ Construct principles for metastrategic focus within the learning experience.
   - ❏ Construct decontextualized principles for bridging.
   - ❏ Share bridging examples that connect to decontextualized principles and learning to a setting outside the present experience.

Checklist of CEA Teacher-Mediator Qualities

The purpose of the Checklist of CEA Teacher-Mediator Qualities is to help teacher-mediators internalize the many aspects of mediated learning and provide them with an opportunity to reflect on their strengths and weaknesses as mediators of the learning experience.

A Look at the CEA Teacher-Mediator

Effective CEA teacher-mediators need to incorporate qualities into mediated learning experiences beyond the four essential ones of reciprocity, intent, meaning, and transcendence. The inclusion of these additional qualities depends on such circumstances as the needs of individual learners and the context in which mediated learning takes place. This is where the art and science of mediated learning truly come together. The checklist can help teacher-mediators focus on the characteristics and roles of an effective mediator.

The checklist has three sections, focusing on the qualities of a teacher-mediator when serving as a leader of mediated learning experiences, ensuring that the four essential qualities actually occur; as a facilitator of mediated learning experiences, striving to establish a laboratory for learning within the classroom; and as a joiner of mediated learning experiences, engaging with students as another learner.

Although teacher-mediators always try to facilitate rather than transmit learning, this facilitation occurs on a continuum from the teacher-mediator as leader to joiner. There are certainly times in any classroom when it is very appropriate to lead the learning. At other times, the focus is much more on general facilitation of the learning process. At still other times, teacher-mediators can best function as a joiner in the learning process with students.

Leader of Mediated Learning Experiences

The first portion of the checklist asks teachers to assess their leadership qualities in the laboratory for learning, including the essential qualities of effective mediators: reciprocity, intent, meaning, and transcendence (see chapter 2 for a discussion of these qualities). This portion of the checklist also evaluates two other areas: challenge, the ability to modify lessons appropriately to help put learners in their zone of proximal development, and task regulation, the ability to plan and organize the learning experience and how events take place within it.

Facilitator of Mediated Learning Experiences

As facilitators, teacher-mediators help students focus on the learning process by assisting them in developing insight into various concepts that can help them learn how to learn in any situation. Assessment of teacher-mediators in this area appears under the heading metastrategic knowledge development. As facilitators of the learning process, teacher-mediators need to help students use the Tools of Self-Regulation and Self-Change almost all of the time. Because Self-Regulation is more encompassing than the other Tools and Building Blocks and teachers need to emphasize its use along with Self-Change more often, these Tools appear in the checklist.

This portion of the checklist also asks teachers to reflect on their use of process-oriented activities because facilitators of the learning process must modify learning activities so students can focus on the learning process and require less leading by the teacher. Facilitators also help the entire classroom community interact in ways that allow everyone to feel safe enough to share openly, offer only as much assistance as students need, and help students help each other, so the checklist assesses open classroom atmosphere and supportive learning opportunities.

Joiner of Mediated Learning Experiences

At times, teacher-mediators must step out of the role of leader or even facilitator to become another learner in the classroom community, inquiring into the learning process. To join successfully with students in the classroom community, teacher-mediators must be involved emotionally with other learners, share personal learning experiences openly, and seek shared understanding or joint regard of a personal worldview with other learners. Under the headings affective involvement, shared experiences, and joint regard, this portion of the checklist asks teachers to reflect on these skills.

Completing the Checklist

As the checklist is a detailed reference document, teachers should not attempt to address it in its entirety in a single period of reflection. Rather, it is best to focus on a few aspects at a time. Items on the checklist were determined based on a review of literature, including, but not limited to, the theory of mediated learning experience. The checklist was also adapted from Lidz's Mediated Learning Experience Rating Scale as it was revised for use in CEA research (1991).

Teacher-mediators can use the checklist in a variety of ways. Some teacher-mediators prefer to use it for self-reflection, rating themselves on each item, checking off those qualities they use frequently or noting those qualities they do not yet have in their repertoire. Other teacher-mediators use the checklist in partnership with one or more other teacher-mediators, either talking about their individual use of certain mediator qualities or as a means for reflecting together while watching videotapes of the interactions each has facilitated in the classroom. In some situations, school staff members have asked CEA consultants and coordinators to observe their classrooms and complete the checklist to provide feedback.

The rating system the checklist employs asks teacher-mediators to make a precise evaluation of their strengths and weaknesses in each area; however, teachers need not use the numbers. The purpose of the checklist is to provide teachers with reflection topics and give them areas to focus on to strengthen their role as mediators and improve the success of their laboratory for learning.

After responding to the questions, teacher-mediators should think about why a particular score is low and what they can do to improve the response. Are the higher scores in areas they feel more comfortable in? How can they bring that comfort level to other areas? Is the "failure" in their activities? In their response to students? In their understanding of the Building Blocks and Tools? A discussion of the results with colleagues often yields valuable advice on how other teachers improved an area of weakness.

Checklist of CEA Teacher-Mediator Qualities

TEACHER-MEDIATOR AS LEADER

1. **Reciprocity:** adjusting one's interaction to learners' cues and signals

   Rate on a scale of 1 (rarely) to 4 (almost always).

   _____ 1.1 Responds appropriately to student cues

   _____ 1.2 Responds in a timely manner to student cues

   _____ 1.3 Balances the involvement of more active and passive students in the learning experience

   _____ 1.4 Changes the focus of meaning and transcendence as needed to ensure student active involvement and ownership of the ideas

2. **Intent:** focusing student attention on the selected purpose for the learning experience, as modified by student ownership of the intent

   Rate on a scale of 1 (rarely) to 4 (almost always).

   _____ 2.1 Shares objectives and goals for the learning experience

   _____ 2.2 Monitors student attention on specific parts of the learning experience

   _____ 2.3 Focuses on reasons for paying attention

   _____ 2.4 Checks for student ownership of the intent

   _____ 2.5 Modifies intent to allow for student ownership of the intent

3. **Meaning:** energizing awareness and making the experience personally relevant

   Rate on a scale of 1 (rarely) to 4 (almost always) the degree to which teacher-mediator helps students find personal significance for the learning experience.

   _____ 3.1 Highlights and animates various aspects of the learning experience through voice, gesture, and movement

   Rate the following items higher if students rather than teacher-mediator generate the information.

   _____ 3.2 Explores the personal relevance of the learning experience by helping students describe the relationship between their prior knowledge and new concepts

   _____ 3.3 Explains with facts why highlighted concepts within the learning experience are important

_____ 3.4 Explains with opinions why certain concepts within the learning experience are important

_____ 3.5 Establishes relationships among thoughts and events occurring within the learning experience

4. **Transcendence:** going beyond the immediate context to make a decontextualized connection between some principle or idea and its use in other contexts in prior and future learning situations

   Rate on a scale of 1 (rarely) to 4 (always). Rate higher if students generate the information.

   _____ 4.1 Connects prior or future events to the present learning experience

   _____ 4.2 Uses hypothetical thinking to make connections among events inside and outside the learning experience

   _____ 4.3 Describes relationships among concepts and connects events within the learning experience and those of the subject matter at a broader level

   _____ 4.4 Engages students in formulating decontextualized principles derived from the relationships within the learning experience as they apply in general, outside the present context

   _____ 4.5 Helps students focus on the process of learning related to the learning experience rather than the product

5. **Challenge:** maintaining the learning experience at a level where the task demands are neither too low and boring nor too high and frustrating

   Rate on a scale of 1 (rarely) to 4 (almost always), focusing on student involvement.

   _____ 5.1 Selects challenging activities that require students to reach beyond their current level of functioning

   _____ 5.2 Asks challenging questions that require students to reach beyond their current level of functioning

   _____ 5.3 Modifies learning experiences for appropriate level of challenge based on an ongoing needs assessment

   _____ 5.4 Engages students in accepting responsibility for their personal learning in the given situation

6. **Task Regulation:** monitoring and guiding what occurs during the learning experience

   Rate on a scale of 1 (low degree) to 4 (high degree) of appropriate level of regulation and involvement of students.

   _____ 6.1 Guides the learning experience in a coherent direction

_____ 6.2   Engages students in developing a plan or sequence of activities for the learning experience

_____ 6.3   Engages students in explaining why the plan is helpful for learning

_____ 6.4   Modifies the plan based on needs displayed by students within the learning experience

TEACHER-MEDIATOR AS FACILITATOR

1. **Metastrategic Knowledge Development:** building a shared vocabulary for reflecting on cognitive processes that foster effective thinking (Building Blocks) and affective-motivational approaches (Tools) that foster independent and interdependent learning

   Rate on a scale of 1 (rarely) to 4 (almost always). Rate higher if students generate the information.

   _____ 1.1   Provides insight into the need for one or more Building Blocks and Tools in this and other learning experiences

   _____ 1.2   Encourages use of one or more Building Blocks or Tools to build personal learning strategies within the learning experience

   _____ 1.3   Engages students in bridging specific Building Blocks or Tools to other contexts

2. **Self-Regulation:** thinking about thoughts and actions as they occur to make needed changes regarding an approach to a learning experience

   Rate on a scale of 1 (low) to 4 (high) degree to which teacher-mediator facilitates student generation of information

   _____ 2.1   Explains how to monitor thoughts and actions during the learning process

   _____ 2.2   Encourages students to monitor their thoughts and feelings during the learning process

   _____ 2.3   Encourages students to monitor the speed at which they work during the learning process to monitor efficiency and impulsiveness

   _____ 2.4   Encourages students to monitor their exploration, planning, and expression of ideas within the learning experience

   _____ 2.5   Encourages students to make needed changes in their approach to a learning experience based on their monitoring

3. **Self-Change:** understanding the difference between what one knows and can do before and after a learning experience

   Rate on scale of 1 (low) to 4 (high) degree to which teacher-mediator facilitates student generation of this information.

   _____ 3.1   Engages students in describing the difference in their level of understanding before and after a successful learning experience

   _____ 3.2   Engages students in describing the difference in what they can do before and after a successful learning experience

4. **Process-Oriented Activities:** selecting, adapting, or creating materials and activities that enhance the learning process

   Rate on a scale of 1 (rarely) to 4 (almost always).

   _____ 4.1   Selects and develops activities that require students to integrate ideas

   _____ 4.2   Selects and develops activities that allow students to make choices regarding some parts of the activities

   _____ 4.3   Selects and develops activities that have more than one appropriate response

   _____ 4.4   Selects and develops activities that focus attention on the process of learning at least as much as the product

   _____ 4.5   Selects and develops activities that promote active involvement of all students simultaneously within the learning experience

   _____ 4.6   Selects and develops activities that connect school learning to the real world

5. **Open Classroom Atmosphere:** establishing a learning environment in which students feel safe to explore and construct new knowledge

   Rate on a scale of 1 (low) to 4 (high) degree to which teacher-mediator and all students exhibit an open atmosphere.

   _____ 5.1   Demonstrates high expectations for all students to learn

   _____ 5.2   Demonstrates respect for all efforts to learn regardless of whether students display mastery

   _____ 5.3   Encourages thinking that leads to effective learning

   _____ 5.4   Treats the classroom as a laboratory for learning rather than a stage for producing right answers

   _____ 5.5   Values and acts on learning opportunities that occur when students display problems

   _____ 5.6   Avoids co-opting a learning opportunity

_____ 5.7 Helps students accept and cope with the common occurrence of learning problems throughout life by highlighting examples of problems for learners of all ages and emphasizing what might have or did overcome the problems

_____ 5.8 Helps students understand and value learning by highlighting examples of effective, independent and interdependent, lifelong learning.

6. **Supportive Learning Opportunities:** responding to student learning problems in a manner that provides opportunities for everyone to receive or give appropriate assistance needed to promote personal growth and to avoid co-opting student learning opportunities

Rate on a scale of 1 (low) to 4 (high) the quality of facilitating individual learning.

_____ 6.1 Provides wait-time during learning experiences (except during rote memory learning) to allow all students time to think

_____ 6.2 Focuses attention on what was said or done so students with problems can evaluate their response before receiving any assistance

_____ 6.3 Assures students with problem that not knowing how to do something is acceptable when students are willing to use an approach that can help overcome the learning problem

_____ 6.4 Provides only as much assistance as needed, usually by gradually increasing the amount of assistance based on observed need for more

_____ 6.5 Displays the four essential qualities of mediating learning experiences within the assistance

_____ 6.6 Engages students in describing an approach to overcoming the given learning problem, usually involving use of a strategy based on a Building Block or Tool

_____ 6.7 Provides assistance by suggesting, or having others suggest, a way to approach the task, usually involving a stratcgy based on a Building Block or Tool

_____ 6.8 Provides prompts and clues to assist students in responding

_____ 6.9 Models the desired response

_____ 6.10 Encourages students by commenting on the way they engage in the learning process

_____ 6.11 Provides descriptive feedback that is immediate, specific, and credible

_____ 6.12 Provides an opportunity for students to share a response at the time the problem occurred or later, even if the response is one of repeating the response of the teacher or another student

TEACHER-MEDIATOR AS JOINER

1. **Affective Involvement:** positive emotional attachment to students

   Rate on a scale of 1 (rarely) to 4 (almost always).

   _____ 1.1 Interacts warmly with students through friendly facial expressions and display of enthusiasm, sincerity, trust, and acceptance

   _____ 1.2 Communicates a feeling of enjoying being with the students

2. **Shared Experiences:** communicating thoughts, feelings, and experiences to others

   Rate on a scale of 1 (rarely) to 4 (almost always).

   _____ 2.1 Shares feelings and thoughts about personal experiences as a learner, such as learning from one's own mistakes

   _____ 2.2 Shares feelings and thoughts related to feelings and thoughts shared by students

   _____ 2.3 Engages students in sharing their experiences as learners

   _____ 2.4 Engages students in thinking about other people's experiences as learners

3. **Joint Regard:** sharing an experience or personal worldview among several learners

   Rate on a scale of 1 (rarely) to 4 (almost always).

   _____ 3.1 Strives to understand students' perspective and personal worldview related to the learning experience

   _____ 3.2 Acknowledges students' perspective with comments that allow students to become aware of listeners' misunderstandings and correct them

   _____ 3.3 Encourages students to join the teacher as collaborative learners

Reflection on Building Blocks and Tools

This section contains self-reflection exercises for teachers and students. Teacher-mediators can use the following list to generate topics for a reflective journal entry.

Teacher-Mediator Self-Reflection on Use of Building Blocks of Thinking and Tools of Learning

1. Describe a Building Block of Thinking or Tool of Learning in your own words as it relates to your personal use.

2. Describe a Building Block of Thinking or Tool of Learning in your own words as it relates to your students' use.

3. Describe an example of a student's effective or ineffective use of a Building Block or Tool.

4. Describe as objectively as you can a situation in which you had difficulty mediating a Building Block or Tool.

5. Describe the feelings you had in the situation described in #4.

6. Think about your use of a Building Block or Tool in the classroom over the past few days. Describe an event that has meaning for you.

7. Create a mindmap of concepts related to a Building Block or Tool.

8. Create a mindmap of insights gained by your students related to a Building Block or Tool.

9. Describe a learning problem one or more students in your class displays. Reflect on the relationship of the problem to one or more Building Blocks and Tools.

10. Reflect on your vision for your students related to their learning to learn.

Student Self-Reflection on Use of Building Blocks of Thinking and Tools of Learning

Each reflection form focuses on student use of one Building Block of Thinking or Tool of Learning within a given learning activity. Teachers can use the student self-reflection forms to encourage students to think about their use of Building Blocks and Tools, to help students set goals for improving their use of Building Blocks and Tools, to create a record of student perceptions over time to keep in a portfolio, and to send home with students to complete with the help of family members.

Each form has five statements. Following each statement is a line with the word Effective on one side and Ineffective on the other. Students mark how effective or ineffective they think they were regarding the given statement on a specific assignment or activity. It is very difficult to reflect on use across many different activities; however, students can complete reflections on the same day regarding their use of a Building Block or Tool in two subject matter areas such as reading and math and compare the differences. No learner uses Building Blocks or Tools equally well in all areas of learning. These comparisons help students build a Feeling of Competence about their ability to use them more effectively in other settings.

The forms also include a final statement where students write their personal goals for improving their use of the Building Block or Tool. They can base these goals on one of the preceding five statements. Teachers can reproduce the forms and use them as often as teacher-mediators and students find appropriate.

Modify the language of the reflection sheets for younger students and those with limited reading skills, or read them aloud with students the first several times students complete a reflection.

The schedule for use of the reflection forms depends on laboratory for learning needs. Typically, students use a form for one Building Block or Tool at a given time; most likely when it is the focus of minilessons. Students can also use the forms as part of the introduction of a Building Block or Tool or on the last day a Building Block or Tool is the main focus in the classroom. Students may also select a Building Block or Tool of their preference for reflection.

The reflection forms should not replace journal writing for reflecting on the use of Building Blocks and Tools. Rather, their purpose is as a catalyst for deeper reflections during journal writing, to allow for a more objective record of change over time, and to provide a review of the various aspects of each Building Block and Tool. Keep copies in folders to which students have access when they want to review past reflections.

Reflections on My Use of the CEA Building Block of Thinking

EXPLORATION

Name: _____   Date: _____

While I was doing

_____

1. I thought about what I needed to know before I started to work.

   Effective . . . . Ineffective

2. I listened carefully before I answered questions.

   Effective . . . . Ineffective

3. I gathered all the information or supplies I needed before I began to work.

   Effective . . . . Ineffective

4. I searched for information or supplies in an organized way.

   Effective . . . . Ineffective

5. I thought carefully about what others said before I shared my thoughts.

   Effective . . . . Ineffective

I will improve my use of Exploration by

_____

_____

_____

_____

165

Reflections on My Use of the CEA Building Block of Thinking

PLANNING

Name: _____   Date: _____

While I was doing

_____

1. I determined the outcomes I wanted for my work.

   Effective . . . . Ineffective

2. I decided what steps to take to reach my outcomes.

   Effective . . . . Ineffective

3. I decided the order of the steps I planned.

   Effective . . . . Ineffective

4. I changed my plan when something did not work.

   Effective . . . . Ineffective

5. I thought of reasons each step was necessary and reasons I should or should not change my plan.

   Effective . . . . Ineffective

I will improve my use of Planning by

_____

_____

_____

_____

Reflections on My Use of the CEA Building Block of Thinking

EXPRESSION

Name: _____   Date: _____

While I was doing

_____

1. I communicated clearly what I wanted to express in this activity.

    Effective . . . . Ineffective

2. I used my plan as I communicated my thoughts and actions.

    Effective . . . . Ineffective

3. I expressed everything needed to make my response effective.

    Effective . . . . Ineffective

4. I expressed my thoughts and actions in the order I intended to express them.

    Effective . . . . Ineffective

5. I expressed my thoughts and actions without co-opting the opportunity of others to learn.

    Effective . . . . Ineffective

I will improve my use of Expression by

_____

_____

_____

_____

Reflections on My Use of the CEA Building Block of Thinking

WORKING MEMORY

Name: _____   Date: _____

While I was doing

_____

1. I used information stored in my brain to help me think.

    Effective . . . . Ineffective

2. I cleared thoughts and feelings from my working memory that would keep
    me from learning effectively.

    Effective . . . . Ineffective

3. I focused energy on the thoughts I needed in my working memory.

    Effective . . . . Ineffective

4. I tried to use all the space I could in my working memory.

    Effective . . . . Ineffective

5. I focused energy in my working memory on storing important information
    in my brain.

    Effective . . . . Ineffective

I will improve my use of Working Memory by

_____

_____

_____

_____

Reflections on My Use of the CEA Building Block of Thinking

MAKING COMPARISONS

Name: _____   Date: _____

While I was doing

_____

1.   I knew there was a need for Making Comparisons all the time during this activity.

   Effective . . . . Ineffective

2.   I made comparisons automatically while I worked.

   Effective . . . . Ineffective

3.   I thought about ways two or more objects, ideas, or actions were the same
     or different.

   Effective . . . . Ineffective

4.   I compared my thoughts and actions with what I expected them to be.

   Effective . . . . Ineffective

5.   I found my careless mistakes by comparing what I did with what I meant to do.

   Effective . . . . Ineffective

I will improve my use of Making Comparisons by

_____

_____

_____

_____

Reflections on My Use of the CEA Building Block of Thinking

GETTING THE MAIN IDEA

Name: _____   Date: _____

While I was doing

_____

1. I thought automatically about Getting the Main Idea while I worked.

    Effective . . . . Ineffective

2. I thought about what the bits of information had in common.

    Effective . . . . Ineffective

3. I was aware of the need to think about Getting the Main Idea to learn effectively.

    Effective . . . . Ineffective

4. I tried to see how objects, ideas, and actions were related to each other.

    Effective . . . . Ineffective

5. I talked with others to see if we agreed about the main idea.

    Effective . . . . Ineffective

I will improve my use of Getting the Main Idea by

_____

_____

_____

_____

Reflections on My Use of the CEA Building Block of Thinking

THOUGHT INTEGRATION

Name: _____   Date: _____

While I was doing

_____

1. I thought about the need to combine bits of information while I worked.

    Effective . . . . Ineffective

2. I combined some bits of information to form a whole idea.

    Effective . . . . Ineffective

3. I combined some bits of information in the correct sequence to form an idea.

    Effective . . . . Ineffective

4. I combined all the bits of information necessary to form an idea.

    Effective . . . . Ineffective

5. I shared my whole ideas with others.

    Effective . . . . Ineffective

I will improve my use of Thought Integration by

_____

_____

_____

_____

Reflections on My Use of the CEA Building Block of Thinking

CONNECTING EVENTS

Name: _____   Date: _____

While I was doing

_____

1. I thought about the need for Connecting Events while I worked.

    Effective . . . . Ineffective

2. I thought about how this activity relates to events that happened in the past.

    Effective . . . . Ineffective

3. I thought about how this activity relates to events that might happen in the future.

    Effective . . . . Ineffective

4. I thought about how to use what I know about other events to help me learn in this activity.

    Effective . . . . Ineffective

5. I shared my connections with others.

    Effective . . . . Ineffective

I will improve my use of Connecting Events by

_____

_____

_____

_____

Reflections on My Use of the CEA Building Block of Thinking

PRECISION AND ACCURACY

Name: _____   Date: _____

While I was doing

_____

1. I thought about the need for Precision and Accuracy while I worked.

   Effective . . . . Ineffective

2. I found appropriate ways to seek a precise understanding of words and concepts.

   Effective . . . . Ineffective

3. I was able to get a precise understanding when I needed to understand words and concepts better.

   Effective . . . . Ineffective

4. I was able to use words and concepts accurately when expressing my ideas.

   Effective . . . . Ineffective

5. I helped others get a precise understanding of words and concepts.

   Effective . . . . Ineffective

I will improve my use of Precision and Accuracy by

_____

_____

_____

_____

Reflections on My Use of the CEA Building Block of Thinking

SPACE AND TIME CONCEPTS

Name: _____ Date: _____

While I was doing

_____

1. I thought about space concepts of size that I needed in my work.

   Effective . . . . Ineffective

2. I thought about space concepts of shape that I needed in my work.

   Effective . . . . Ineffective

3. I thought about space concepts of distance that I needed in my work.

   Effective . . . . Ineffective

4. I thought about how events happen in time.

   Effective . . . . Ineffective

5. I thought about sequencing ideas as needed in my work.

   Effective . . . . Ineffective

I will improve my use of Space and Time Concepts by

_____

_____

_____

_____

Reflections on My Use of the CEA Building Block of Thinking

SELECTIVE ATTENTION

Name: _____ Date: _____

While I was doing

_____

1. I decided what was important to think about as I worked.

   Effective . . . . Ineffective

2. I decided what information was irrelevant to my work.

   Effective . . . . Ineffective

3. I focused attention on relevant information.

   Effective . . . . Ineffective

4. I ignored irrelevant information.

   Effective . . . . Ineffective

5. I helped others use Selective Attention.

   Effective . . . . Ineffective

I will improve my use of Selective Attention by

_____

_____

_____

_____

175

Reflections on My Use of the CEA Building Block of Thinking

PROBLEM IDENTIFICATION

Name: _____   Date: _____

While I was doing

_____

1. I thought about the need to use Problem Identification.

    Effective . . . . Ineffective

2. I experienced a feeling of imbalance when a problem occurred.

    Effective . . . . Ineffective

3. I defined problems that I experienced.

    Effective . . . . Ineffective

4. I experienced and defined problems automatically.

    Effective . . . . Ineffective

5. I helped others use Problem Identification effectively.

    Effective . . . . Ineffective

I will improve my use of Problem Identification by

_____

_____

_____

_____

Reflections on My Use of the CEA Tool of Learning

INNER MEANING

Name: _____ Date: _____

While I was doing

_____

1. I thought about why this work is important to me.

    Effective . . . . Ineffective

2. I thought about why this work is interesting to me.

    Effective . . . . Ineffective

3. I thought about why this work is useful for me to do.

    Effective . . . . Ineffective

4. I thought about how this work relates to my world outside of school.

    Effective . . . . Ineffective

5. I encouraged others to find their Inner Meaning.

    Effective . . . . Ineffective

I will improve my use of Inner Meaning by

_____

_____

_____

_____

Reflections on My Use of the CEA Tool of Learning

FEELING OF CHALLENGE

Name: _____   Date: _____

While I was doing

_____

1. I thought about the feelings I was having about how challenging this work was to do.

    Effective . . . . Ineffective

2. I focused my attention on feelings about challenge that made my learning more fun and exciting.

    Effective . . . . Ineffective

3. I took my attention away from feelings of anxiety or fear about challenge.

    Effective . . . . Ineffective

4. I broke into parts what was challenging me.

    Effective . . . . Ineffective

5. I thought about what I already knew that could help with this challenge.

    Effective . . . . Ineffective

I will improve my use of Feeling of Challenge by

_____

_____

_____

_____

Reflections on My Use of the CEA Tool of Learning

AWARENESS OF SELF-CHANGE

Name: _____ Date: _____

While I was doing

_____

1. I thought about how I have changed in my ability to do this work.

   Effective . . . . Ineffective

2. I thought about how I expect to change because of learning to do this work.

   Effective . . . . Ineffective

3. I thought about how important it is for me to change.

   Effective . . . . Ineffective

4. I understood the feelings I had about my change.

   Effective . . . . Ineffective

5. I am aware that I have changed in the past and will change more in the future.

   Effective . . . . Ineffective

I will improve my use of Awareness of Self-Change by

_____

_____

_____

_____

179

Reflections on My Use of the CEA Tool of Learning

FEELING OF COMPETENCE

Name: _____   Date: _____

While I was doing

_____

1.   I thought about how important it is to feel secure about my ability to do this work.

   Effective . . . . Ineffective

2.   I thought about skills I have that would help me do this work.

   Effective . . . . Ineffective

3.   I thought about how important it is to develop positive beliefs about my ability to do this work.

   Effective . . . . Ineffective

4.   I used information about my ability to do this work to feel more competent.

   Effective . . . . Ineffective

5.   I helped others build a Feeling of Competence.

   Effective . . . . Ineffective

I will improve my use of Feeling of Competence by

_____

_____

_____

_____

Tools

Reflections on My Use of the CEA Tool of Learning

SELF-REGULATION

Name: _____   Date: _____

While I was doing

_____

1. I thought about my thoughts and actions while they were occurring.

    Effective . . . . Ineffective

2. I made changes in the way I approached the learning experience based on this special thinking.

    Effective . . . . Ineffective

3. I used Self-Regulation to help me think about Building Blocks and Tools I could use to work more effectively

    Effective . . . . Ineffective

4. I developed learning strategies to help solve my problems based on this special thinking.

    Effective . . . . Ineffective

5. I regulated how fast I worked based on how complex and how familiar the work is and how much time I needed to do well with this kind of work.

    Effective . . . . Ineffective

I will improve my use of Self-Regulation by

_____

_____

_____

Reflections on My Use of the CEA Tool of Learning

GOAL ORIENTATION

Name: _____ Date: _____

While I was doing

_____

1. I set goals for myself.

   Effective . . . . Ineffective

2. I persisted in working toward my goals.

   Effective . . . . Ineffective

3. I reached the goals it was possible to reach while doing this work.

   Effective . . . . Ineffective

4. I kept working toward my goals even when it was difficult.

   Effective . . . . Ineffective

5. I shared my goal-oriented behavior with others.

   Effective . . . . Ineffective

I will improve my use of Goal Orientation by

_____

_____

_____

_____

Reflections on My Use of the CEA Tool of Learning

SELF-DEVELOPMENT

Name: _____ Date: _____

While I was doing

_____

1. I thought about what I can do best in relation to this work.

    Effective . . . . Ineffective

2. I worked on goals related to my strengths to develop them more.

    Effective . . . . Ineffective

3. I thought about what I don't do so well that keeps me from using my strengths effectively.

    Effective . . . . Ineffective

4. I worked on goals related to improving in ways that let me use my strengths more effectively.

    Effcctive . . . . Ineffective

5. I helped others see how much I appreciate their strengths.

    Effective . . . . Ineffective

I will improve my use of Self-Development by

_____

_____

_____

_____

Reflections on My Use of the CEA Tool of Learning

SHARING BEHAVIOR

Name: _____   Date: _____

While I was doing

_____

1. I shared my thoughts and actions with others.

   Effective . . . . Ineffective

2. I listened carefully to what others said.

   Effective . . . . Ineffective

3. I asked questions that helped me better understand the thoughts of others.

   Effective . . . . Ineffective

4. I tried to learn from the ideas of others.

   Effective . . . . Ineffective

5. I tried to learn new information by combining my thoughts with those of others.

   Effective . . . . Ineffective

I will improve my use of Sharing Behavior by

_____

_____

_____

_____

BLACKLINES

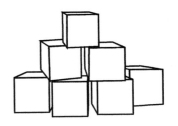

Exploration

Gather information systematically

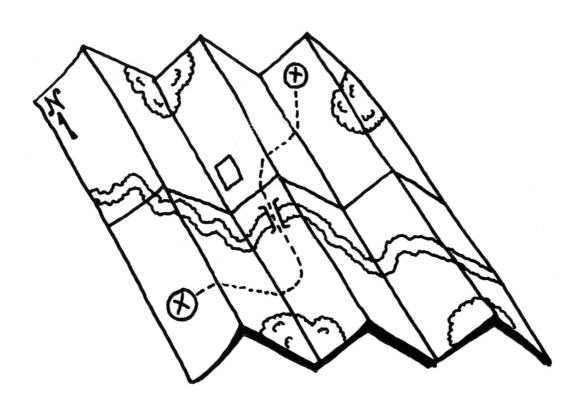

Planning

Use an organized approach

Expression

Communicate clearly and with control

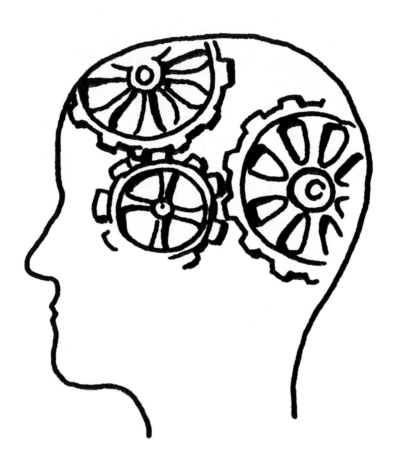

Working Memory

Use memory processes effectively

Making Comparisons

Discover similarities and differences

Getting the Main Idea

Identify the basic thought

Thought Integration

Combine pieces of information

Connecting Events

Find relationships among learning experiences

Precision and Accuracy

Understand and use words and
concepts correctly

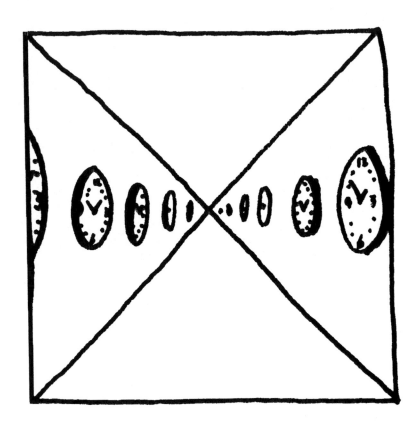

Space and Time Concepts

Understand and use
space and time information

Selective Attention

Focus on relevant information

Problem Identification

Experience an imbalance
when a problem occurs

Inner Meaning

Seek personal value in learning

Feeling of Challenge

Manage reactions to new
and complex learning

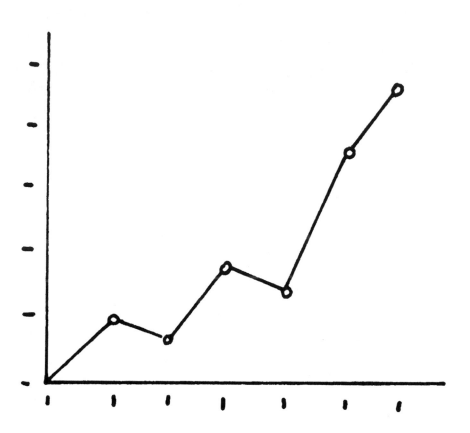

Awareness of Self-Change

Recognize and welcome personal growth

Feeling of Competence

Energize learning by feeling
secure about abilities

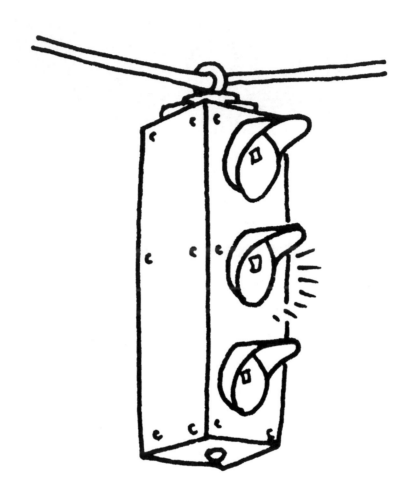

Self-Regulation

Reflect on thoughts and actions

Goal Orientation
Take purposeful action

Self-Development

Appreciate everyone's qualities

Sharing Behavior

Share thoughts and actions

Glossary

Advisory board A group of educators and family members who serve as leaders in making decisions about family-school partnerships and other CEA areas. In CEA, the Advisory Board facilitates the building of a shared purpose that all families and educators have ownership in.

Affect Attitudes, values, and feelings related to learning. In CEA, four Tools of Learning focus on understanding feelings that impact independent and interdependent learning.

Affective-motivational approaches Parameters of mediated learning that lead to effective integration of feelings and use of processes that energize learning behavior. In CEA, Tools of Learning are affective-motivational approaches learners can use to build personal learning strategies to understand feelings and motivate behaviors in learning experiences.

Approaching the learning experience Exploring, planning, and expressing thoughts and actions.

Awareness of self-change To recognize and understand feelings related to personal growth and to learn to expect and welcome change and development. A CEA Tool of Learning for understanding feelings in the learning experience.

Bridging A technique for connecting the use of a Building Block or Tool in one setting to its use in other settings by means of development of a general principle that applies in all settings. In CEA, bridging helps students transfer metastrategic knowledge to home, school, work, and social settings.

Building blocks of thinking Cognitive process of effective thinking learners can use to develop personal learning strategies. The twelve Building Blocks of Thinking focus on approaching, making meaning, or confirming the learning experience.

CEA consultant A professional certified to offer CEA professional development activities and support to schools and families using the program

Closed classroom atmosphere A classroom environment in which students are expected to produce one right answer, and product is valued over process. (Contrast with open classroom atmosphere.)

COGNET The original name of the Cognitive Enrichment Advantage. COGNET stands for Cognitive Enrichment Network Education Model.

Cognitive approach A cognitive education teaching method that focuses on student acquisition of learning strategies designed by experts to apply to specific tasks such as reading comprehension or mathematics problem solving. (Contrast with metacognitive approach and metastrategic approach.)

Cognitive deficiencies Ineffective learning habits that develop when learners do not use cognitive processes effectively.

Cognitive processes Specific prerequisites to thinking. In CEA, the Building Blocks of Thinking are cognitive processes learners can use to create personal learning strategies to assist in problem solving, decision making, and approaching, making meaning, and confirming learning experiences.

Collaborative learning Learning that takes place among two or more people, where ideas develop that belong to the group rather than any one individual. Collaborative learning focuses on inquiry over advocacy of ideas and suspending assumptions so group members can explore the ideas of all members.

Confirming the learning experience Clarifying, validating, correcting, and defining needs.

Connecting events To find relationships automatically among past, present, and future learning experiences. A CEA Building Block of Thinking for making meaning of the learning experience.

Cooperative learning A classroom approach for group activities that uses four basic principles: 1. appropriate need to share knowledge across group members, 2. accountability for the contributions of all group members, 3. equal balance of participation across group members, and 4. opportunity for all to engage in active learning at the same time. In CEA, cooperative learning is combined with collaborative learning and the use of a metastrategic approach, often resulting in more effective learning, inquiry, and successful engagement in highly challenging and motivating learning.

Co-opting To take away another person's learning opportunity. (See also supportive learning opportunities.)

Cultural transmission Sharing one's worldview with others, especially children for which one is a caregiver or teacher. According to Feuerstein, caregivers are motivated to share cultural values and ways of knowing and doing, which results in the natural occurrence of mediated learning experiences.

Decontextualized Taken out of context. Generalized in a way that transfers to many different contexts. In CEA, bridging principles are decontextualized so they apply to many situations in home, school, work, and social settings.

Domain A subject matter focus. A specified area of study.

Exploration To search systematically for information needed in the learning experience. A CEA Building Block of Thinking for approaching the learning experience.

Expression To communicate thoughts and actions carefully in the learning experience. A CEA Building Block of Thinking for approaching the learning experience.

Family-school partnership An approach to furthering interaction between family members and school staff. In CEA, family-school partnerships emphasize shared purpose, respect for family members and school staff expertise, and equality within the partnership. Together, family members and educators can help students develop pride in their home culture, respect for the culture of others, and an understanding of school expectations.

Feeling of challenge To energize learning in new and complex experiences effectively. A CEA Tool of Learning for understanding feelings in the learning experience.

Getting the main idea To identify spontaneously the basic thought that holds related ideas together. A CEA Building Block of Thinking for making meaning of the learning experience.

Goal orientation To take purposeful action in consistently setting, seeking, and reaching personal objectives. A CEA Tool of Learning for motivating behavior in the learning experience.

Independent learning Taking responsibility for thinking, remembering, and learning for oneself. In CEA, it involves using Building Blocks of Thinking and Tools of Learning effectively without needing others to remind one to do so.

Inner meaning To seek deep, personal value in learning experiences that energizes thinking and behavior and leads to greater commitment and success. A CEA Tool of Learning for understanding feelings in the learning experience.

Inquiry learning Learning that occurs through exploring, accommodating, and assimilating information to which one is directly exposed. It depends on the ability to learn independently. It involves open-ended activities, opportunities for critical thinking, and the testing of personal theories. In CEA, inquiry learning is always used in conjunction with a metastrategic approach so underachieving and nontraditional learners have a much better chance of learning successfully.

Intent Catching or focusing attention within a mediated learning experience. This quality belongs to the mediator.

Interdependent learning Learning that takes place when all involved contribute to a learning outcome they would not achieve in the same way without everyone's contributions. CEA encourages interdependent learning through collaborative and cooperative learning opportunities and the laboratory for learning classroom.

Laboratory for learning Student-centered learning environment in which the teacher and students form a learning community and explore the world together in personally relevant ways. Members of the laboratory for learning socially construct knowledge through interaction with each other. Focus is on the process of learning at least as much as the product. The teacher guides but does not control the conversation, which balances inquiry with advocacy of ideas. Teachers also help students learn how to learn. Self-regulation is valued over teacher regulation of behavior. (Contrast with traditional learning environment.)

Learning school An approach to helping students gain an understanding of the hidden rules of school culture. The greater the gap between the school culture and the student's personal worldview and home culture, the greater the need for learning school.

Learning strategies Specific plans for improving some aspect of the learning process. In CEA, students develop personal learning strategies rather than memorize and use an expert learning strategy the teacher provides. Students develop plans that apply some aspect of a Building Block of Thinking or Tool of Learning that they believe can help them improve their process of learning in that situation or addresses specific learning problems.

Making comparisons To discover similarities and differences automatically among some parts of the learning experience. A CEA Building Block of Thinking for making meaning of the learning experience.

Making meaning of the learning experience Retrieving, comparing, synthesizing, relating, integrating, and comparing ideas.

Meaning Energizing awareness and making the learning experience personally relevant. This quality belongs to the mediator. The learner needs to develop inner meaning to be effective in any learning experience.

Mediated learning experience A sharing of cultural meanings and values through a reciprocal relationship between a learner and more knowledgeable others. Mediators focus learners' attention on specific ideas, energize the interaction with meaning relevant to learners, and help learners decontextualize ideas so learners can apply them beyond the current learning experience.

Memory Processes in the brain that allow storage and retrieval of information and its integration with new ideas. (See also working memory.)

Metacognition Awareness of one's own thinking processes and monitoring one's thoughts and actions as they occur. (See also Self-Regulation.)

Metacognitive approach A cognitive education teaching method that helps students determine their need for learning strategies and plan and monitor their use of expert learning strategies. (Contrast with cognitive approach and metastrategic approach.)

Metastrategic approach A cognitive education teaching method that helps students plan and monitor their use of personally developed learning strategies and reflect on alternative strategies. This is the CEA approach to cognitive education that involves students in building a shared vocabulary for reflecting on cognitive processes that foster effective thinking (Building Blocks of Thinking) and affective-motivational approaches (Tools of Learning) that foster independent and interdependent learning. (Contrast with cognitive approach and metacognitive approach.)

Metastrategic knowledge Understanding cognitive processes and affective-motivational approaches to learning that learners can use to develop personal learning strategies. In CEA, metastrategic knowledge focuses on explicit understanding of cognitive processes as reflected in Building Blocks of Thinking and of affective-motivational approaches to learning as reflected in Tools of Learning.

Mindmap A graphic organizer that visually organizes important concepts and their relationships to each other.

Minilessons The CEA professional development tool that helps teachers facilitate students' understanding and use of Building Blocks of Thinking and Tools of Learning. Minilessons also provide guidance for integrating Building Blocks and Tools into curricular lessons.

Motivating behavior within the learning experience Choosing, initiating, and persisting in specific actions

Motivation The energizing force that drives behavior related to learning. In CEA, four Tools of Learning focus primarily on motivating behavior that leads to effective independent and interdependent learning.

Open classroom atmosphere A classroom environment in which students feel accepted, safe, and appropriately challenged. They are willing to share their learning and seek assistance in the process of learning and how to improve it. Most activities involve choice and student input into evaluation and encourage experimentation. A laboratory for learning includes an open classroom atmosphere. (Contrast with closed classroom atmosphere.)

Personal learning strategies (See metastrategic approach and learning strategies.)

Planning To prepare and use an organized approach in the learning experience. A CEA Building Block of Thinking for approaching the learning experience.

Precision and accuracy To know there is a need to understand words and concepts and use them correctly and to seek information automatically when the need arises. A CEA Building Block of Thinking for confirming the learning experience.

Principle A decontextualized rule. A generalization. In CEA, principles are an important aspect of the technique of bridging.

Problem identification To experience a sense of imbalance automatically and define its cause when something interferes with successful learning. A CEA Building Block of Thinking for confirming the learning experience.

Reciprocity A positive connection of acceptance, trust, and understanding between the learner and the mediator. An essential quality of mediated learning experiences, it greatly impacts the effectiveness of the other essential qualities (intent, meaning, and transcendence).

Schemas Interconnected ideas and beliefs stored in memory that provide an understanding of how to function in the world.

Selective attention To choose between relevant and irrelevant information and to focus on the information needed in the learning experience. A CEA Building Block of Thinking for confirming the learning experience.

Self-development To appreciate special qualities in everyone and to enhance personal potential. A CEA Tool of Learning for motivating behavior in the learning experience.

Self-efficacy Beliefs based on perceptions of one's experiences and ability to perform that connect motivation and cognition. Also called self-schema. Self-efficacy may or may not match the actual ability and understanding one has in a given area, and the beliefs may help or interfere with learning and performance.

Self-reflection Careful consideration of one's thoughts and actions. CEA encourages self-reflection as a means of self-evaluation to determine the effective use of metastrategic knowledge and how one might change one's use of Building Blocks of Thinking and Tools of Learning.

Self-regulation To reflect on thoughts and actions as they occur to energize, sustain, and direct behavior toward successful learning and doing. A CEA Tool of Learning for motivating behavior in the learning experience.

Self-schema (See self-efficacy.)

Sequential processing A cognitive process of coding that involves the consideration of data in a series, one bit of information after the other. Also called successive processing. (Contrast with simultaneous processing.)

Sharing behavior To energize life and learning for everyone by sharing thoughts and actions through effective interdependent learning skills. A CEA Tool of Learning for motivating behavior in the learning experience.

Simultaneous processing A cognitive process of coding that involves the synthesis of pieces of information into a combined whole. (Contrast with sequential processing.)

Social construction of knowledge Process of learning that assumes members of their social group influence learners' construction of knowledge. Knowledge and understanding moves among people, and learners eventually assimilate and accommodate them. In CEA, mediated learning experiences are thought to influence greatly the social construction of knowledge.

Space and time concepts To understand and use information about space and time that is important in almost all learning. A CEA Building Block of Thinking for confirming the learning experience.

Supportive learning opportunities Responding to student learning problems in a manner that provides opportunities for everyone to receive or give appropriate assistance needed to promote personal growth and to avoid co-opting student learning opportunities.

Systemic change An approach to change that considers the many hidden influences and interrelated connections that must be addressed to bring about effective change efforts.

Teacher-mediator Anyone serving in the role of teacher in a learning situation who uses the CEA comprehensive teaching approach.

Thought integration To combine pieces of information into a complete thought and hold onto them while needed. A CEA Building Block of Thinking for making meaning of the learning experience.

Tools of learning Affective-motivational approaches to learning that learners can use to understand their feelings and motivate their behavior in learning experiences by building personal learning strategies based on them.

Traditional learning environment Teacher-centered instruction where the teacher selects learning activities with minimal input from students. The teacher provides instruction and determines how well students can memorize, transfer, and apply the information imparted to them. The teacher controls conversation, students are expected to provide the one right answer, and teachers regulate behavior rather than focus on the need for self-regulation. (Contrast with laboratory for learning.)

Transfer The ability to apply what one learns in one setting to other settings.

Transcendence Expanding understanding beyond the context of the current learning experience. Going beyond the immediate needs in a learning experience to make a decontextualized connection between ideas and their use in other contexts. This essential quality of mediated learning experiences belongs to the mediator.

Understanding feelings within the learning experience Optimizing the positive effect of emotions that accompany thoughts and actions and impact values.

Users' network A CEA approach to facilitate the ongoing development of an international, supportive, and expanding network that enables family members, educators, and others to provide and receive mutual support as they seek to maximize learning potential for all students

Working memory To use memory processes effectively. The term describes memory processes that include clearing distractions from the mind, focusing energy on thinking, remembering and retrieving old information, and integrating and storing old and new information in the brain. It is also a CEA Building Block of Thinking for making meaning of the learning experience. (See also memory.)

Worldview A frame of reference and way of knowing based on cultural beliefs and implicit, or hidden, rules for how to think and act.

Zone of proximal development According to Vygotsky, the interval within which a person can continue to learn in a given situation only if another, more knowledgeable other, provides assistance.

References

Arrien, A. 1993. *The fourfold way: Walking the paths of the warrior, teacher, healer, and visionary.* San Francisco: Harper.

Ashman, A.F., and R.N.F. Conway. 1997. *An introduction to cognitive education: Theory and applications.* New York: Routledge.

Brofenbrenner, U. 1991. Comments at symposium, Conference of Academic Researchers on Youth Museum Practices, Indianapolis, Indiana.

Bruffee, K.A. 1993. *Collaborative learning: Higher education, interdependence, and the authority of knowledge.* Baltimore: Johns Hopkins University Press.

Bruner, J. 1982. The language of education. *Social Research,* 49:835–853.

Coulter, M., and K.H. Greenberg. 1994. Unraveling the mysteries of learning to learn: Research and issues. In *Changing children's minds,* 2nd ed., edited by H. Sharon and M. Coulter. Birmingham, England: Sharon Publishing.

Covey, S.R. 1989. *The 7 habits of highly effective people: Restoring the character ethic.* New York: Simon & Schuster.

Dale, P.S., and K.N. Cole. 1988. Comparison of academic and cognitive programs for young handicapped children. *Exceptional Children,* 54:439–447.

Das, J.P., J.A. Naglieri, and J.R. Kirby. 1994. *Assessment of cognitive processes: The PASS theory of intelligence.* Boston: Allyn & Bacon.

Eggen, P., and D. Kauchak. 1997. *Educational psychology: Windows on classrooms.* 3rd ed. Westerville, OH: Merrill.

Feuerstein, R., Y. Rand, and M.B. Hoffman. 1979. *The dynamic assessment of retarded performers: The learning potential assessment device, theory, instruments, and techniques.* Glenview, IL: Scott Foresman.

Feuerstein, R., Y. Rand, M.B. Hoffman, and R. Miller. 1980. *Instrumental enrichment: An intervention program for cognitive modifiability.* Baltimore, MD: University Park Press.

Feuerstein, R., M.R. Jensen, M.B. Hoffman, and Y. Rand. 1985. Instrumental enrichment: An intervention program for structural cognitive modifiability. In *Thinking and learning skills, Vol. 1, Relating instruction to research,* edited by J. Segal, S. Chipman, and R. Glaser. Hillsdale, N.J.: Lawrence Erlbaum.

Feuerstein, R., P.S. Klein, and A. Tannenbaum. 1990. *Mediated Learning Experience (MLE): Theoretical, psychosocial, and learning implications.* London: Freud Publishing House, Ltd.

Fullan, M. 1993. *Change forces: Probing the depths of educational reform.* London: Falmer Press.

Garcia, T., and P.R. Pintrich. 1994. Regulating motivation and cognition in the classroom: The role of self-schemas and self-regulatory strategies. In *Self-regulation of learning and performance: Issues and educational applications,* edited by D.H. Schunk and B.J. Zimmerman. Hillsdale, N.J.: Lawrence Erlbaum.

Greenberg, K.H. 1990. Mediated learning in the classroom. *International Journal of Cognitive Education and Mediated Learning,* 1:33–44.

Greenberg, K.H. 1992. *Research and mediated learning: Implications for program implementation.* Paper presented at conference, Mediated Learning in Health & Education: Forging a New Alliance. Tampa, Florida.

Greenberg, K.H. 1995. *Evidence of effectiveness: The COGNET education model.* (Unpublished.) University of Tennessee, Knoxville.

Greenberg. K.H. 2000. *The cognitive enrichment advantage family-school partnership handbook.* Arlington Heights, IL: SkyLight Professional Development.

Greenberg, K.H., L. Coleman, and W. Rankin. 1993. The cognitive enrichment network program: Goodness of fit with gifted underachievers, *Roeper Review,* 2:91–95.

Greenberg, K.H., M. Woodside, and L. Brasil. 1994. Differences in the degree of mediated learning and classroom interaction structure for trained and untrained teachers. *Journal of Classroom Interaction,* 29(2):1–9.

Greenberg, K.H., S. Machleit, and A. Schlessmann-Frost. 1996. *Cognitive enrichment network education model (COGNET).* Urbana, IL: ERIC Clearinghouse on Elementary and Early childhood Education. Resources in Education (RIE). (PS024949)

Greenfield, S.A., ed. 1996. *The human mind explained: An owner's guide to the mysteries of the mind.* New York: Henry Holt & Co.

Hall, G. 1975. *LoU chart: Operational definitons of levels of use of the innovation.* Austin, TX: Research and Development Center for Teacher Education, University of Texas.

Hargrove, R. 1995. *Masterful coaching.* San Francisco: Jossey-Bass.

Hargrove, R. 1998. *Mastering the art of creative collaboration.* New York: McGraw-Hill.

Hawkins, D. 1974. *The informed vision: Essays on learning and human nature.* New York: Agathon.

Haywood, C. 1994. *Leveling the playing field: The critical importance of mediated learning in intervention programs.* Paper presented at the eleventh annual meeting of the California Association for Mediated Learning, Oxnard, California.

Heath, S.B. 1983. *Ways with words.* Cambridge: Cambridge University Press.

Heller, M.F. 1986. How do you know? Metacognitive modeling in the content areas. *Journal of Reading,* 29:415–422.

Henderson, R.W., and L. Cunningham. 1994. Creating interactive sociocultural environments for self-regulated learning. In *Self-regulation of learning and performance: Issues and educational applications,* edited by D.H. Schunk and B.J. Zimmerman. Hillsdale, N.J.: Lawrence Erlbaum.

Henry, W.A. III. 1992. The century ahead: Ready or not here it comes! *Time,* Special Issue, Fall:36.

Hundeide, K. 1991. *Helping disadvantaged children: Psycho-social intervention and aid to disadvantaged children in third world countries.* London: Jessica Kingsley.

Jarvis, P. 1992. *Paradoxes of learning.* San Francisco: Jossey-Bass.

Kagan, S. 1992. *Cooperative learning.* San Juan Capistrano, CA: Resources for Teachers, Inc.

Kendall, P.C., and L. Braswell. 1985. *Cognitive behavior therapy for impulsive children.* New York: Guilford Press.

Klein, P. S. 1995. *Early intervention: Cross-cultural experiences with a mediational approach.* Vol. 887, Garland Reference Library of Social Science. Levittown, PA: Garland.

Klein, P.S., and S. Alony. 1993. Immediate and sustained effects of maternal mediating behaviors on young children. *Journal of Early Intervention,* 17:177–193.

Lidz, C.S. 1991. *Practitioner's guide to dynamic assessment.* New York: Guilford Press.

Maurer, R. 1996. *Beyond the wall of resistance.* Austin, TX: Bard Books.

Mayer, R.C. 1988. Learning strategies: an overview. In *Learning and study strategies: Issues in assessment, instruction and evaluation,* edited by C. Wienstein, E. Goetz, and P. Alexander. New York: Academic Press.

McCombs, B.L. 1989. Self-regulated learning and academic achievement: A phenomemological view. In *Self-regulated learning and academic achievement: Theory, research, and practice,* edited by D.H. Schunk and B.J. Zimmerman. New York: Springer.

Mook, D.G. 1996. *Motivation: The organization of action.* 2d ed. New York: W.W. Norton & Company.

National Assessment of Educational Progress. 1990. *The Reading Report Card, 1971–1988: Trends from the Nation's Report Card.* Washington, DC.

Ogle, D.M. 1986. KWL: A teaching model that develops active reading of expository text. *The Reading Teacher,* 396:564–570.

Perkins, D.N., and G. Salomin. 1989. Are cognitive skills context-bound? *Educational Researcher,* January/February:16–25.

Peters, J. 1991. Strategies for reflective practice. In *Professional development for educators of adults,* edited by R. Brockett. San Francisco: Jossey-Bass.

Piaget, J. 1976. *The grasp on consciousness.* Cambridge: Harvard University Press.

Presseisen, B. Z., and A. Kozulin. 1992. *Mediated learning: The contributions of Vygotsky and Feuerstein in theory and practice.* Paper presented at the annual meeting of the American Educational Research Association, San Francisco.

Presseisen, B.Z., B. Smey-Richman, and F.S. Beyer. 1993. Cognitive development through radical change: Restructuring classroom environments for students at-risk. In *Creating powerful thinking in teachers and students: Diverse perspectives,* edited by J.N. Mangieri and C.C. Block. New York: Harcourt Brace.

Schunk, D.H., and B.J. Zimmerman, eds. 1994. *Self-regulation of learning and performance: Issues and educational applications,* Hillsdale, N.J.: Lawrence Erlbaum.

Senge, P.M. 1993. *The fifth discipline: The art and practice of the learning organization.* New York: Doubleday.

Senge, P.M.; A. Kleiner, ed; C. Roberts, G. Roth, and R. Ross. 1999. *The dance of change.* New York: Doubleday.

Shotler, J. 1993. *Cultural politics of everyday life: Social constructionism, rhetoric, and knowing of the third kind.* Toronto: University of Toronto Press.

Smith, F. 1986. *Insult to intelligence.* Arbor House: New York.

Vygotsky, L. 1978. *Mind in society: The development of higher psychological processes.* Cambridge: Harvard University Press.

Weir, S. 1989. The computer in schools: Machine as humanizer. *Harvard Educational Review,* 59: 61–73.

Wigfield, A. 1994. The role of children's achievement values in the self-regulation of their learning outcomes. In *Self-regulated learning and academic achievement: Theory, research, and practice,* edited by D.H. Schunk and B.J. Zimmerman. New York: Springer.

Index